THE PRIVATE

JOSH COHEN is Professor of Modern Literary Theory at Gold-smiths, University of London and a psychoanalyst in private practice. He is the author of books and articles on modern literature, cultural theory and psychoanalysis, including *How to Read Freud* (Granta, 2005).

'Doubling as a literary academic and a psychoanalyst, Josh Cohen is well poised to engage in acts of interpretation – of texts, patients, the culture as well as himself. In *The Private Life*, he examines some of the tensions in our snooping- and celebrity-obsessed world, where privacy is in danger of becoming a dirty word' Lisa Appignanesi, *Observer*

'Josh Cohen has written an interesting book, which is both topical and original' Karl Miller, founder of the *London Review of Books*

'Reflective, dark and literary . . . Cohen touches a nerve. His use of literature, his autobiographical vignettes and his reflections on his own psychoanalytic experiences gradually seduce one into his mode' *Jewish Quarterly*

'What Cohen brings to this debate is a caution that understanding another person is simply a matter of pulling down the dissembling veil that separates us from each other' Giles Fraser, *Guardian*

'This makes for fascinating reading, and the arguments are examined from a range of perspectives. *The Private Life* is an enjoyable and witty read, and one that will probably make you reconsider the habit of lifelogging' *We Love This Book*

'Enlightening without being sententious . . . *The Private Life* deserves a place on domestic shelves to be read and referred to again and again, and every time to provide something new to think about' *Jewish Chronicle*

Josh Cohen

The Private Life

Why We Remain in the Dark

GRANTA

Granta Publications, 12 Addison Avenue, London W11 4QR

First published in Great Britain by Granta Books, 2013
Paperback edition published by Granta Books, 2014

A CIP catalogue record for this book is available from the British Library.

1 3 5 7 9 10 8 6 4 2

ISBN 978 1 84708 530 6

Typeset by Avon DataSet Ltd, Bidford on Avon, Warwickshire

Printed and bound by CPI Group (UK) Ltd, Croydon, CR0 4YY

To my family

Contents

Introduction

I'm in the sparsely populated carriage of an Overground train. As we crawl into Euston, the realization that I'm the sole audience to a woman a few seats in front, tearfully berating a man on her mobile phone, tears me out of my reverie. 'It's over,' she tells him through heaving sobs. 'Don't you fucking talk to me. I fucking hate you. Why? Don't you fucking give me why, you stinking bastard. Don't pretend you don't know. Don't pretend, don't, don't you fucking pretend.' All her murderous despair throbs in her thumb as she terminates the call. She leans her head against the window, still volubly crying. I gaze out the opposite side, heat creeping up my face. I tell myself I'm an involuntary witness to another's lack of emotional inhibition, conveniently passing over my own rapt interest in the scene.

Several minutes later I'm hovering in front of the magazine racks in Smith's. I stare glassily at the covers of *Heat*, *Closer*, *Reveal*, the titles amplifying the promise of furtive proximity intimated in the hazy shots below. An arrow tagged *Serious tummy!* points to the slack flesh spilling over the bikini bottom of a soap actress hunched on the edge of a sun lounger. Another, aimed at the ribcage pressing through the skin of a bikini-clad TV presenter, asks *Dangerously skinny?!* Something about the distracted obliviousness of their postures and expressions seems more obscene than anything the dead-eyed glamour models nearby can conjure. Too self-conscious to browse, I shuffle out, taking with me only my mild shame.

These unexceptional few moments have revealed to me my participation, at once resentful and willing, in a culture of intrusion, held together by the unholy alliance of voyeurism and exhibitionism. The first principle of this culture, upheld by wire taps and telephoto lenses on the one hand and by the pervasive casual display of personal intimacies on the other, is that I should know everything. Nothing, from the near side to the furthest reaches of bodily and emotional experience, should be kept from view. As those few minutes showed me, it's hard to opt out of this culture and the malevolent excitement it stirs up.

Many celebrities and other public figures rightly protest against this culture, but their lamentations for their lost privacy only feed the spectacle they want to escape. Nothing seems better calculated to provoke an assault on privacy than the plea to respect it.

What accounts for this relentless war on our own and others' privacy? What, exactly, are we attacking? No doubt our envy is never far away, our wish to despoil the beauty, wealth, fame, talent and love another enjoys more than us by ensuring they'll never really enjoy it. And so we lurch blindly between the idealization of airbrushed glamour and the humiliation of candid telephoto shots, caught in a vindictive rage to exhaust every possible form of the celebrity's visibility. And why? What is this compulsive gorging on images of the same body and clothes and lovers and excesses?

It's as though we're caught in the furious suspicion, amplified with every image, that we're missing something, that the very thing we're looking for is being withheld, that there are places beyond us no telephoto lens or bugging device can reach. The guiding principle of our culture might be formulated not so much as 'I should know everything' as 'nothing should remain unknown to me'. It's not, in other words, a question of wanting to know so much as a fear of what might remain unknown, inaccessible, in the dark.

The conception of privacy implicit in public debates around the competing rights of individual and public interest is a rather impoverished one, mired in the confusion of privacy with secrecy. Privacy is framed in terms of the secrets I may wish to unearth and you may wish to withhold – your sexual or financial affairs, for example. This idea of private life can be reduced to what you might call bourgeois privacy, the privacy of what you do or own. When politicians, lawyers and journalists argue about privacy their focus is typically on those facts of external life you might prefer to keep to yourself. *We can keep secret*, writes the philosopher Martin Heidegger, *only what we know*. But isn't there another, more essential privacy, namely what I keep private even from myself – and in spite of myself? Drag every sordid secret into the light and something of your self, perhaps the very thing that really matters, would still remain in the dark. It's the privacy of this stubborn remainder, which no lens can penetrate and no law can defend, that I shall explore in this book.

Books provided my first intuitions of this obscurity in the self. My avid consumption of poetry, novels and comics, unabated since early childhood, began in my fascination for the strangeness of other people's voices. I read books obsessively, and eventually chose to teach them, because they hinted at the miraculous possibility of experiencing inner lives other than my own. Weeks into my undergraduate degree I read Freud, and immediately felt a deep and visceral affinity for his description of psychic life.

But I was never much drawn to psychoanalytic literary criticism, to shedding the light of the unconscious, transferences or drives on the dark enigmas of poems and novels. My relationship to psychoanalysis felt somehow too private for that kind of generalized application. Freud's *Dora*, the first case history I read, showed me that psychoanalysis, for all its theoretical richness, was rooted not in speculative abstractions, but in a risky and unpredictable encounter between two live human beings.

I didn't know what to do with this conviction that psychoanalysis didn't live in texts alone, until I met a practising psychoanalyst many years later. Here was someone whose daily life, at once like and radically unlike mine, orbited around the experience of other voices and the struggle to listen to what they were saying. Within a few weeks of meeting him I'd embarked on my own analysis and eventually on the long and difficult journey to becoming an analyst. Psychoanalytic training was at once a radical departure from and a continuation of the same personal project, a new way of tuning in to other voices – not least other voices in myself.

The first premise of psychoanalysis is that the very existence of a private zone of inner life – what psychoanalysis calls the unconscious – is so unbearable that we spend much of our lives and energies denying it. I came across this insight in books; but it was only the long experience of being on and behind the couch that enabled me to feel rather than merely know it as true.

The consulting room revealed to me in particular the profound irony that our passion to know is at the same time a passion not to know. This double passion says a lot about today's culture of pathological intrusiveness. Perhaps the demand that nothing remain unknown is directed less towards everyone else than towards ourselves. The right we assert to know everything about everyone else may be nothing less than an unconscious protest against our ignorance of ourselves.

This may give us a clue as to why the hunger for scandalous revelation is so insatiable. Gossip is always dated. As soon as it gains a new piece of knowledge, it casts it aside in ruthless pursuit of what it doesn't yet know. Gossip simultaneously tantalizes you with the possibility of knowing all and fuels the suspicion that something is always irremediably lacking in your knowledge, that however much you know, you'll always fall short. Psychoanalysis hints that your voracious wish to know everything is tied intimately to the humiliating truth that you can't know everything. You are, in other words, destined to an ignorance you'll never overcome – a suggestion for which psychoanalysis receives much scorn and contempt, and just occasionally some gratitude and relief.

The possibility that there may be something that you not only don't know (which can always be remedied) but can't know, and which nonetheless is at the heart of who and what you are, is peculiarly affronting. The instinctive response to the impudent suggestion that you're not who you think you are is to bristle indignantly and insist that *you* will have final say on who you are and aren't. Freud famously characterizes this bristling as the consequence of the third in a trio of blows that science would deal to humankind's vanity across the centuries. The first of these was the Copernican displacement of the Earth from the centre to the periphery of the cosmos. The second was Darwin's discovery of the human's biological roots in the non-human animal. But *human megalomania will have suffered its third and most wounding blow from the psychological research of the present time* [i.e. psychoanalysis] *which seeks to prove that the ego is not even master in its own house, but must content itself with scanty knowledge of what is going on unconsciously in its mind.* As Freud saw it, human beings are bound to experience this curtailment of their unlimited right and capacity to know, and more particularly to know about themselves, as a wound that defies healing.

In contemporary culture, celebrities have become the target of collective rage against this humiliation. By intruding into their bedrooms, bodies and bank accounts, the media and its consumers – that is, all of us, more or less – seek to penetrate and destroy not simply *their* privacy, but privacy itself. The very existence of a life unseen is a scandal to be eliminated at all costs. The veil celebrities cast on their lives behind the scenes works as a permanent provocation to tear through it, to defy the limit it tries to place on what we can know. The tantalizing fascination and peculiar genius of the reality TV celebrity Katie Price lie in her engineering of a cult around precisely this play of the assertion and defiance of privacy. The ongoing striptease she performs on her deepest secrets, promising the full monty of revelation that is never quite delivered, initially relieves and finally exacerbates the humiliation of our wish to know everything, a humiliation that morphs imperceptibly into masochistic pleasure.

The possibility that celebrity culture is a kind of drama around the scope and limits of what can be known leads me to wonder if it isn't a kind of folkish counterpart to the modern scientific spirit. Writing in 1938 (and during the period of Nazi affiliation that would forever disgrace his troublingly great philosophical legacy) in one of a series of lectures on the logic of modern science and technology, Heidegger declared that *the fundamental event of the modern age is the conquest of the world as picture*. In other words, for modern science (and Heidegger is referring here to all forms of knowledge, not just to the natural sciences), the world exists only as a collection of objects to be classified and quantified. Whatever can't be quantified or *pictured* is effectively consigned to non-existence.

But Heidegger suggests that the most fundamental truth of existence itself – the fact of Being – cannot be quantified or reduced to a thing among things. What he gnomically calls *the forgetting of Being* is the failure of science to take account of the very ground of the world and everything in it. There's something, you could say, that's always in excess of what can be known and communicated, a kind of private life in the very heart of the world around you, which induces in modern science an enraged defiance.

'Nothing should remain unknown to us' is the guiding formula of modern science as much as of media culture. Technologies in the fields of genetics, neuroscience, pharmacology and atomic physics are promising to put an end to the unknown, finding answers to questions that had seemed for millennia to be irresolvably enigmatic: the origins of the universe, the nature of human and animal life and consciousness, the structure of space and time. Technology and science are putting the world under their sway, ensuring that nothing is beyond their reach.

Don't we see this spirit at work in the zealous war led by Richard Dawkins and others against the stubborn persistence of religion? The fury religion induces in its opponents may be less about its particular content than its premise of a necessary limit to knowledge. Modern science will tolerate no challenge to its own sovereignty, and to imply one is likely to be heard as a scandal. From the perspective of the New Atheism, religion is a kind of systematic subjection of the universe to the rule of ignorance. Its blindness, and Dawkins would no doubt fail to appreciate the comparison, is the inexplicably wilful blindness Christianity once ascribed to the Jews, a persistence in denying the irrefutable evidence of eye and mind. And as with the Jews in traditional Church doctrine, this can't simply be put aside as the opponent's own affair. For its contemporary critics, religion isn't merely a comically inferior mode of thinking to be left to its own devices, but a persistent affront to it, a mischievous pretender to its territory, claiming for ignorance what science must win for knowledge.

In scientific and media culture alike, nothing unknown can remain thus. Neither self nor world can be granted the right to privacy. Zones of obscurity, where knowledge fails to reach, are sources of fear and contempt, demanding no less than elimination. In this book, I offer claims for psychoanalysis, art and ordinary human experience as ways into a different relationship to our own and others' privacy.

If you have nothing to hide, you have nothing to fear, runs the menacing slogan of our inexorably creeping culture of monitoring and surveillance. The problem is that you always have something to hide, and so something to fear. There is an obscure yet essential region in you, suggests the British psychoanalyst D. W. Winnicott, that can survive only by remaining hidden, and whose natural elements are darkness and silence. This mute spot in your interior is the very source of your creative life, and to intrude into it, suggests Winnicott, is the most profound violation a person can experience. Our culture's flooding of the world with light, its unrelenting promotion of our permanent visibility, is in danger of making this profound violation a routine fact of daily life. As our anxious concern for the privacy of our personal property and data intensifies, the quiet surrender of the privacy of our selves goes unnoticed.

1

The Voice in the Dark

The boy narrator of Patrick Ness's remarkable young adult novel of 2008, *The Knife of Never Letting Go*, lives in a dystopian New World in which he's assailed at every moment by *the Noise*, the involuntary broadcast of each person's thoughts to everyone else. *The Noise*, Todd tells us, *is a man unfiltered, and without a filter, a man is just chaos walking*. The novel begins with his dangerous discovery of *a hole in the Noise*, a small pocket of privacy in which your thoughts are audible to no one but yourself.

Perhaps there is an allegory of the Noise that has overtaken our own everyday lives in this premise, and more particularly of a social networking culture that tacitly coerces people into the perpetual broadcast of their external and internal selves. But it also triggers thoughts less specific to our cultural present, of the universal need for an inviolable private space.

When I stumbled on it recently, the book aroused a long-dormant memory from age four, perhaps five, of one of my many sleep-over visits to my grandparents' home. Far from dystopian, these visits to the large yet homely mock-Tudor house were interludes of unbroken indulgence, in which all desires, for play or rest but above all for food, were anticipated and fulfilled before I had the chance even to name them. The overflowing bowls of tenderly stewed button mushrooms and buttered macaroni and thick cinnamon-dusted almond custard, their smells wafting seductively through the house, transformed the round Formica kitchen table into a small boy's harem.

In my over-sated haze, I would quietly wonder whether my grandmother could hear what I wanted before I did. For the most part, this had the dreamy quality of a uterine regression. But I wonder if, on the visit in question, I wasn't starting to feel some inchoate need for a filter on the noise of my childish wishes, a guilty resistance to being so exhaustively known.

One morning, following the usual salty-sweet banquet, I wandered over to my favourite room in the house. My grandfather's study was divided from the den by a retractable door, a massive pane of thickly ridged glass set in a wooden frame, through which you could make out the rusty blur of packed, jacketless book spines lining the back wall from floor to ceiling. Sliding the door open and shut with a heave, I made for my favoured spot, a low leather stool in the back left-hand corner, and let myself be held in its noiseless embrace.

The moment I heard my grandmother call my name, I felt a reflexive twitch in my knees. When my legs failed to follow through, I drew breath to call back to her, only to hear my own silence. It dawned on me that, without quite knowing why, I wasn't going to move or make a sound. Having found my hole in the Noise, I wasn't going to surrender it on demand.

Over the next five or six minutes, I sat in the fog of my stubborn inertia, which only entrenched itself more deeply the more irritable, then concerned, then desperate became her cries of my increasingly biblical-sounding name. By the time she found me, her wailing and gnashing of teeth had reached such a pitch as to make her fury indistinguishable from her relief.

Perhaps this is a story of the ruthless infantile sadism you prefer to forget about as your childhood fades from memory, of a mutinous reversal of power in which I made the overbearingly loving adult feel the humiliating sting of helpless dependency. Or perhaps that's just the idle retrospective gaze of the psychoanalyst. If I try to feel my way into the scene, all I can sense in my child self is a will to cling to the sides of this hole, this transient corner of inalienable privacy.

In my determination to remain in hiding, to screen out the sound of my own name, I hear a protest against being too readily identified, the mute insistence that not even my grandmother should know everything about me. Was I dimly aware that my grandfather's absence was on account of leading prayers in the synagogue at the end of the road, to the same God I'd just heard my grandmother calling on for help? Perhaps I was intuiting an insight of religion, an insight that would crystallize many years later when I discovered psychoanalysis – that there is a core of experience that defies certain knowledge.

Psychoanalysis is not religion. But for many scientists and philosophers, it presents the same provocation, namely its insistence on the limits of knowing. Neither religion nor psychoanalysis has comported itself, through their respective histories, in the spirit of humility implied by this limit on knowledge. Many justifiably see both as embodying the arrogance of those who think they have all the answers (though psychoanalytic disputes haven't yet sparked bloody wars and genocides, for all their bitterness and rancour). It's a peculiar irony that two practices that have the unknowable at their core should be so ready to project their omniscience. But perhaps this is the problem with organizing a practice around the unknown: its adherents are liable to appoint themselves sole legitimate guardians and interpreters of the unknown, keepers and masters of the ultimate secrets about ourselves and the world.

The knotted question is how to talk about the unknown without compromising its essential enigma, without turning it into just another fact to be possessed, or else into some quasi-mystical secret vouchsafed only to privileged initiates. It's rather too easy for 'not knowing' to become a rhetorical posture disguising the tacit conviction that of course *I* know, it's just you that doesn't.

One of the more productive paradoxes of psychoanalysis is that it has a very elaborate and systematic theory of the unknowable at the heart of the inner life. Freud, its founding figure, developed this theory, which came to be variously and endlessly augmented, elaborated and contested in the subsequent history of psychoanalysis.

There are dozens of psychoanalytic primers and dictionaries offering definitions of Freud's most fundamental term, the un-conscious. All these definitions point to Freud's location of the unconscious in what he called the 'drives', adding to the sense of terminological obscurity. The drive is an elusive force in us that's neither bodily nor psychical yet both, occupying a no-man's-land that blurs any clear demarcation between the two. Drives are expressions of the human animal's most fundamental internal demands and desires, which Freud, borrowing from Schiller, more than once reduces to the pair 'hunger and love'. They are felt as at once pressures on the body and yearnings in the soul, a mutual internal echo familiar to anyone who's fallen deeply in love, or been consumed by hate or depression or joy or any of the extremities of the inner life.

Freud insisted on the existence of two fundamental drives, the first of which remained constant in his thinking, the second of which changed across the course of his life. The first, with which his name will be forever associated, is the sexual drive, expressed in the peculiarly human energy he called libido. This energy is fundamentally expansive, directed outward from the self to others in the myriad forms of love and desire. In contrast, his first version of the second drive is geared towards self-preservation, to the ego's care of and for itself that Freud calls narcissism, before morphing, in his great and disturbing essay of 1920, *Beyond the Pleasure Principle*, into the death drive, the impulse to return to the state of non-being from which human life first arose.

Sex and death: a drive of erotic expansion outwards, of the creative proliferation of life in all its forms, alongside a drive of nullifying contraction inwards, a depletion of life in the service of silence and inertia. For Freud, the unconscious is an internal space in which these basic impulses express themselves, give voice to their irrational, unruly excess. Internal pressures of this kind, sexual or destructive, are liable to disorganize the mind and body, to unravel the everyday self's precarious cohesion. It's for this reason that they're repressed, kept out of the purview of your conscious mind.

It's easy enough to see the motives for repression when the unconscious is imagined as a container for the most obscure and dangerous internal forces. The unconscious gives you good reasons to keep it unconscious. In their most archaic forms, the impulses to life and death know no bounds; repression puts these bounds in place.

This classical version of the unconscious, essential though it is, hardly exhausts the concept or its subsequent history. Psychoanalysts since Freud have stretched, modified, appended and developed the concept in many different directions. One of the most suggestive of these many developments has been, and continues to be, the work of the contemporary

British (American-born) analyst Christopher Bollas. Building on Winnicott's seminal contributions, Bollas describes an unconscious that operates alongside the Freudian unconscious of drives and their repression. From birth, he suggests, you absorb the styles of being consciously and unconsciously transmitted to you by your adult carers. You internalize in this way not only modes of behaviour – patterns of speech, movement, non-verbal expression – but the full range of inner life. Your infant self is a receptacle of your carers' specific forms of love, hatred, excitement, anxiety, joy and sadness, all of which they transmit to you spontaneously and, so to speak, unthinkingly. In incorporating these modes of feeling and relating, and making them your own, a deep well of unconscious life is installed in you which Bollas calls 'the unthought known'.

In his second book, *Forces of Destiny*, Bollas considers the kind of life that might be worth living in the light of this idea. What he calls a true self resides in this kernel of early infantile experience. But the true self is not some essential, changeless core. In fact, it's not any 'thing' at all, but a repository of possibilities whose realization (or not) will depend on the subsequent course of your experience. *As the true self,* he writes, *is . . . only a potential, it comes into being only through experience.* The mother's (and of course not only the mother's) care implants in her child an unconscious way of being and relating whose shape will evolve and shift according to the course of his life.

The first aim of psychoanalysis is for patient and analyst to establish contact with these two layers of unconscious experience. An analyst attunes himself to the unconscious emanations of sex and death hidden in the patient's verbal and bodily language by listening with his own unconscious. For example, a patient begins the session in prolonged silence before declaring herself exhausted. She can't bring herself to talk, she says, would prefer instead to stay here with her analyst and sleep long and deep. The analyst may hear this in a number of different ways. He may pick up on a deathly impulse in his patient's wish, an urge to drop out of life, to sink into nothingness. Or he may hear, instead of or as well as this refusal of life, a deep erotic wish, a blissful merger (an echo of an infant and her mother), or a playful seduction (the child's earnestly declared fantasy of marrying Mummy or Daddy) of the analyst.

But the meaning of this or any other words of the patient can never be taken for granted, and what the analyst chooses to hear and interpret in them will be heavily influenced by what he picks up from the second layer of unconscious life, the patient's styles of linguistic and bodily expression – their intonation, volume, speed, stillness or agitation. These will evoke in the analyst a sense of his patient's earliest experiences of being loved and hated by, as well as loving and hating, the primary figures in her earliest life. This effort of the analyst to track the foundations of her psychic life gives rise to the famous archaeological metaphor Freud employs to define analytic practice. The psychoanalyst is burrowing down both to the most basic structural level and to the earliest experiences of the mind, searching under the accumulated rubble of the individual's biographical development for the elemental truth of her inner life.

And yet, Bollas points out, the technique by which Freud undertook his research was oddly paradoxical. What he called the 'fundamental rule' of clinical psychoanalysis, namely the practice of free association, whereby the patient follows the trail of the first thought that comes to mind in a given session, is as far as can be from a direct and efficient path to truth. On the contrary, it encourages detours, digressions, improvisations, tellings and retellings of the patient's inner past. Asking who you are and why demands a potentially limitless effort to imagine yourself. Or, in Bollas's words, *To find the truth all patients must lie.* In the psychoanalytic consulting room, truth comes into focus only by following the erring, meandering trails the mind lays down for itself, more often than not without much sense of what it's doing.

The true self makes itself known only through the intricate weave of experience. It's not a discrete object that can be isolated and observed. It reveals itself rather in the ways you make and remake the character transmitted to and internalized by you before you were capable of conscious reflection. These ways of shaping your earliest experience are the path towards realizing your singularity or, Bollas's word, your *idiom* as a self. The practice of psychoanalysis is a means of cultivating this personal idiom, of unearthing the fingerprint that is yours alone.

One important consequence of conceiving the private self as an idiom is that it can no more be equated with an interior than an external self. Your idiom is somehow both openly visible and strangely imperceptible. Walking, smiling, speaking, writing, joking, drawing, eating, weeping, listening – in all these modes of being and doing, you're revealed as at once the most self-evident fact and the most impenetrable secret. Your private self is diffused in all the ways you express yourself, and so isn't reducible to any of them. It's concealed, you could say, less behind than in the face you show the world. You are a secret that hides in plain sight.

A fundamental dilemma, Bollas suggests, bubbles continuously under every human consciousness, occasionally rising urgently to the surface – either to deny your singularity by perceiving your life as fate or to realize it by experiencing it as destiny. The fated person feels entrapped in a story that isn't her own, in a life determined by forces external to her. She experiences the life of a 'false self', led by reactive compliance with the demands of others rather than by her own desires, lived as though it weren't hers to live. The fated person has lost, or failed ever to make contact with, the unconscious sources of her own self. Psycho-analysis is one way of recovering that contact, and of moving from a fateful to a destined conception of oneself.

Two conceptions of the unconscious, then: one which hosts the diverse expressions of the drives, those excessive and obscure forces silently conditioning your manifest self; and one which shelters the unconscious idiom peculiar to you. Far from being competing conceptions, these are inseparable dimensions of unconscious life.

Cultural life, as Freud recognized from the very beginning, is one of the essential ways through which the unconscious makes itself present in individual and collective experience. Take Darren Aronofsky's *Black Swan*, a movie that touched a receptive cultural nerve when it was released in 2010. *Black Swan* can be read as an elaborate meditation on, and expression of, the interplay of these two dimensions of the unconscious. The movie draws us deep into the inner life of Nina Sayers, a young ballet dancer. Nina's technical immaculacy barely conceals her terror of creative spontaneity. Her anxiously coiled perfectionism seems to rule her out of the running for the role of the Swan Queen in his new *Swan Lake*, as far as Thomas Leroy, her flamboyant and predatory choreographer is concerned. She has the grace and poise of the White Swan in abundance, but none of the creative and erotic abandon demanded by the Black Swan. Only her panicked response to his forced kiss – to bite his lip – shocks him into rethinking his decision.

The film's portrayal of Nina's hysterically phobic relationship to her own sexuality and aggression is knowingly overblown. Her environment resounds with perpetual echoes of her strangled inner life: in her creepily desexualized bedroom, its walls lined with angelically white toys, and in the suffocating omnipresence of her mother, whose intrusive solicitousness provides the thinnest veneer for her malevolent envy of her daughter. Even the rehearsal sequences draw you into this constricted inner space, bringing you into uncomfortable and disorienting proximity to the tightly controlled yet oddly precarious movement of her body. In these moments, you enter into her anxious struggle to sustain the machinic precision of her dancing, which no unexpected expression can be allowed to disturb. The idiom of the dancer has to defer to the anonymity of the dance.

But the cracks in Nina's coldly perfect exterior are increasingly visible in the form of hallucinatory glimpses of her double at moments she can't predict. As an anxious Nina, hair severely pulled back, takes hesitant steps towards the subway, her double sashays towards her, loose hair swinging seductively, her expression radiating casual sexual confidence and flashing malevolence in equal measure. This double is shading ever more imperceptibly into the figure of Nina's professional rival and ambiguous friend Lily.

With Nina's double, Aronofsky is drawing on a venerable narrative motif of Western literature, one that's proved insistently fascinating to literary critics and historians as well as psychoanalysts. As Freud recognized in his essay on 'The Uncanny' (and his disciple Otto Rank would confirm in his more expansive study *The Double*), the figure of the double nearly always unleashes a storm of licentiousness and evil. The ensuing chaos can be mined for comedy (as in the *Twins* of the Latin dramatist Plautus, freely adapted by Shakespeare in his *Comedy of Errors*), but in modern literature typically augurs a more sinister atmosphere of internal collapse and mortal danger. From Dostoevsky's *The Double*, Poe's 'William Wilson', Stevenson's *Dr*

Jekyll and Mr Hyde in the nineteenth century, to Auster's *New York Trilogy* or Saramago's *The Double* in our own time, the double is the harbinger of the self's unravelling and destruction. Where the original character feels only horrified alienation in the face of his sexual and destructive impulses, his double brazenly indulges them. The double becomes the container for all the aggression and voluptuousness his original denies.

In his most systematic essay on the unconscious, Freud hints strongly at the unconscious as itself a kind of internal double: *All the acts and manifestations which I notice in myself and do not know how to link up with the rest of my mental life must be judged as if they belonged to someone else: they are to be explained by a mental life ascribed to this person.* In other words, my double becomes the vehicle for expressing an incomprehensible excess in me too frightening to tolerate or even acknowledge.

Nina's hallucinatory confusions derive from her desperate ascription of this excess within her to *someone else*, and in particular to Lily, whom she endows with all the sexual voracity and destructiveness she denies in herself. *Black Swan* also suggests the intimacy of this Freudian unconscious, with the unconscious of the singular self described by Bollas. Thomas Leroy tauntingly equates the frigidity of her movement with its anonymity, its lack of any distinctive bodily or emotional signature. Nina's terror of her sexual and destructive impulses is equally an alienation from her own singularity, her style of being.

The critic and theorist Eric Santner touches on this paradox in his book *Creaturely Life*. The drives bring us into proximity to our animal or 'creaturely' selves, and yet it's precisely when we are most animal that we are most human: *human beings are not just creatures among other creatures but are in some sense **more creaturely** by virtue of an excess . . . that, paradoxically, accounts for their 'humanity'.* As long as Nina keeps herself apart from her creaturely self, projecting it on to real or hallucinated others, she appears coldly inhuman, a stranger to all passions. Only when suicidally merged with her double can she give expression to her singular idiom as a dancer and as a human being. In the film's brilliant last line, *It was perfect*, the dying Nina pays tribute to the final, ecstatic consummation of her creative and destructive impulses, a death which is also the birth of her own singularity. Two conceptions of the unconscious thus erupt in unison at this moment: the 'repressed' unconscious of the drives and the 'unthought' unconscious of the primary or 'true' self. Of course, outside the neo-*Sturm und Drang* world of the film, psychotic delusion and suicide aren't to be idealized as routes to creative self-realization. A more laborious and distinctly less glamorous means of making contact with the different dimensions of the unconscious is to undergo psychoanalysis. Freud saw his new clinical procedure as a method for giving voice to wishes and impulses whose repression had failed, giving rise to unbearable internal conflict and guilt that expressed itself in nervous illnesses – somatic conversions, phobias, obsessional rituals and even paranoid psychoses.

But there is much to suggest that from the first, Freud saw in psychoanalytic method more than a way of inducing his subjects to recognize their inner deviancy. Reading his earliest clinical case histories, set out in the 1895 *Studies on Hysteria*, co-authored with the Viennese physician Josef Breuer, what emerges is the almost accidental discovery of a means of cultivating the patient's own voice.

The *Studies* read as a kind of prehistory of psychoanalytic theory and technique, tracing the faltering path by which Freud arrived at some of his key premises regarding not only hysteria, but the structure and workings of the mind more generally. At its centre are five case histories of female patients, each displaying symptoms of bodily and mental breakdown: disturbances of vision, temporary paralyses, vomiting, auditory and visual hallucinations, tics, phobias, deliria, each frequently accompanied by unexplained pains in one or other part of the body.

These so-called 'neurotic' patients show some markedly borderline and even psychotic features. You might wonder how these women of the fin-de-siècle Viennese haute-bourgeoisie, with their freakish bodily symptoms and crippling social anxieties, could speak to us in the socially and sexually liberated twenty-first-century West as any more than quaint historical curiosities. There may be little resonance for a contemporary reader in the content of these women's stories. And yet something in their histories cuts across the yawning historical gap – less what they say than their struggle to say it. Under Freud's often uncertain gaze, these women are transformed from a sum of intractable symptoms to be resolved into individuals caught inside the impenetrable darkness and incomprehensibility of their own experience, struggling to find some kind of voice, however faltering and incoherent, to make that experience meaningful to themselves and one other. This is the struggle that I bear witness to on an hourly basis in my consulting room and that makes immediate contemporaries of these troubled voices from the distant past.

The second of the cases, 'Miss Emmy von N.', and the first to be treated by Freud (the previous case, Anna O., who would be retrospectively identified as the first psychoanalytic patient, was treated by Breuer), is a widow of forty. When Freud takes her on in spring 1889, she has been suffering from bouts of nervous illness for some fourteen years. She stammers and clasps her fidgety fingers tightly together, while her face and neck jerk in convulsive spasms and her mouth produces persistent involuntary 'clacking' noises. She seems a kind of living attestation to Freud's summary formulation: *the ego is not even master in its own house*. She lives in a state of frightened subjection to the torments inflicted by her own body and mind. Her passivity seems confirmed by her ready assent to Freud's suggestion that she leave her two daughters with their governess and convalesce in a nursing home, where he will visit her every day.

What this and the other case histories in the *Studies* show us is Freud's pained efforts to wrest new ways of thinking about, and with, his patients from the imaginatively constricting terms of established psychiatry. As a relatively young and inexperienced practitioner, he follows the prescribed procedures of his day for treating hysteria in women, in this case the Weir–Mitchell 'cure' (a practice rendered notorious some years later by American feminist Charlotte Perkins Gilman's fictionalized memoir *The Yellow Wallpaper*), in which patients were consigned to an open-ended period of total rest, 'feeding' and a strict moratorium on mental stimulation. To this treatment Freud adds the use of hypnosis as a means of discovering the sources of her symptoms.

For all their differences, both the rest cure and hypnosis intensify the patient's tendency to compliance. Yet what Freud unearths in questioning her under hypnosis is that it's this very tendency that is at the heart of Emmy's illness. In one of their first hypnotic sessions, he asks her about the source of her terrors, and is answered with a memory from her sixth year: *First when I was five years old and my brothers and sisters often threw dead animals at me. That was when I had my first fainting fit and spasms. But my aunt said it was disgraceful and that I ought not to have attacks like that, and so they stopped*. What Emmy recalls, in other words, is a prohibition imposed on her most urgent and overwhelming emotional responses. Internalizing this prohibition has made her ill, torn internally by the conflicting imperatives to express and suppress her states of feeling.

Emmy's imperative to comply inevitably extends into her role as patient. She assents without the slightest demur to her doctor's orders, and proves *an excellent subject for hypnotism*, falling under his spell with the raising of a finger and the order to sleep. Hypnosis, as Freud would come to see, is a means of mastering and coercing the subject's unconscious, of accessing it, as it were, in her absence. The hypnotic state gives Emmy the power of recall over the scenes of death and terror which have been exerting such traumatizing power over her, and enables Freud in turn to *wip[e] away these pictures, so that she is no longer able to see them before her*. Emmy passively submits her unconscious, in other words, to the authority and judgement of the doctor.

But as the treatment continues, something quietly remarkable starts to happen. The material that she produces, both under hypnosis and in her normal waking state, begins to interest Freud as more than a kind of psychic toxic waste that needs to be disposed of. Indeed, in spite of the claims he makes on this score, it seems that what surfaces under hypnosis, far from being wiped from her waking consciousness, is now more readily accessible. The compulsive symptoms with which she once responded to Freud's questioning now give way to complete reproductions of the memories and associated impressions of previous sessions. These recollections, he writes, *often lead on, in a quite unexpected way, to pathogenic reminiscences of which she unburdens herself without being asked to. It is as though she had adopted my procedure and was making use of our conversation, apparently unconstrained and guided by chance, as a supplement to her hypnosis.*

But was this free and undirected talk a mere supplement to the hypnosis? In fact, her spontaneous elaboration of her memories seems to subvert rather than supplement hypnotic suggestion. For the hypnotized subject, there is no traffic between the unconscious and conscious regions of the mind – hypnosis depends for its effectiveness on the latter being made inert, and so on a distinctly authoritarian relationship to the subject's unconscious. In contrast, this moment of *unconstrained* conversation, *perhaps*, as Freud's English translator and editor James Strachey remarks in a footnote, *the earliest appearance of what later became the method of free association*, comes to facilitate a newly self-assertive tone in Emmy's attitude to Freud.

Even under hypnosis she shifts abruptly from her initial attitude of unquestioning submission to at times fierce insubordination. Another hypnotic session sees Freud promise Emmy liberation from the tormenting expectations of misfortune and accompanying physical pains she has been complaining about in recent days. She surprises him by responding spontaneously with the tale of Prince L.'s escape from an asylum and associated rumours of the tortures to which asylum patients are submitted. Freud recalls her having begun a sequence of such horror stories three days previously, only for him to interrupt her. This interruption is suddenly revealed to Freud as a fundamental clinical mistake: *I now saw that I had gained nothing by this interruption and that I cannot evade listening to her stories in every detail to the very end.*

From this point on, Freud finds himself repeatedly on the losing side of a power struggle. She responds to his question about the origins of her stammer with a defiant silence, provoking the following exchange: *'Don't you know?' 'No.' 'Why not?' 'Why not? Because I **mayn't**!'* (*She pronounced these last words violently and angrily.*) She follows this refusal with a demand to be woken out of her hypnosis.

The following session strikes a further blow against Freud's hypnotic authority. He discovers that the *general prohibition* he had placed on her hallucinatory animal deliria by hypnotic suggestion *had been ineffective, and that I should have to take her frightening impressions away from her one by one.* In the process, he asks her about the source of her gastric pains, believing them to accompany the hallucinations. When she replies, *rather grudgingly*, that she does not know, he requests that she *remember by tomorrow*. *She then said in a definite grumbling tone that I was not to keep on asking her where this and that came from, but to let her tell me what she had to say. I fell in with this, and she went on without preface.*

Freud's disciplinary grip becomes ever more tenuous across these sessions. But his achievement, too often neglected by those who charge him with patrician arrogance towards his female patients, is his willingness to embrace his own defeat. Rather than seek to re-exert his control over her, he draws the startling conclusion that he must surrender his authority and submit to the endless flow of Emmy's talk. Nor is there any appeal against her insistent repulsion of his questions. Freud watches helplessly as she furiously dismantles the terms of inquiry he has tried to instate. She effectively forces her way out of his hypnotic control, culminating in her demand that he *let her tell me what she had to say*.

The virtue of Freud's response to this rebellion is that he doesn't think to take it personally. He is, quite simply, too interested in what's happening to worry unduly about his wounded authority as man and doctor. Emmy's insistence that her speech must be allowed to flow uninterruptedly, and her allied refusal to let the doctor set the terms of discussion, become for him sources of insight rather than anxiety. His concern is not to recover his pride, but to explore the possibilities opened up by his humiliation. Out of this imaginative leap comes the realization, at once radically new and breathtakingly simple, that therapy should proceed by the patient telling him what she has to say, and by his listening to her.

This listening will be governed by more than close attention. It will mirror the free, undirected movement of the patient's talk.

Rather than identify in advance the information sought for, or *asking her where this or that came from*, he must wait to hear what she is trying, perhaps without knowing it, to tell him. It is a matter not simply of letting the patient speak her mind, but of letting her mind speak. It demands a stance of receptivity to, rather than control over, the meandering drift of her speech, a stance he will describe seventeen years later as *a surrender to his own unconscious activity*.

Emmy's insistence on Freud listening to her tell what she has to say comes to be heard by him as more than an assertion of her rights as a woman or a patient. She is demanding not only that her suppressed voice be heard, but that it be listened to differently, with an ear unconstrained by existing psychiatric practices which confine and control the body and the imagination alike. She calls for a hearing for the unexpected and unknown in ourselves, for what can be heard only when we don't already know what we're listening for.

Later on in the *Studies*, Freud will discuss the surprising implications of this new mode of speaking and listening for how the case histories of the mentally ill are written about:

> I have not always been a psychotherapist. Like other neuro-pathologists, I was trained to employ local diagnoses and electro-prognosis, and it still strikes me myself as strange that the case histories I write should read like short stories and that, as one might say, they lack the serious stamp of science. I must console myself with the reflection that the nature of the subject is evidently responsible for this, rather than any preference of my own. The fact is that local diagnosis and electrical reactions lead nowhere in the study of hysteria, whereas a detailed description of mental processes such as we are accustomed to find in the

works of imaginative writers enables me to obtain at least some kind of insight into the course of that affection. Case histories of this kind are intended to be judged like psychiatric ones; they have, however, one advantage over the latter, namely an intimate connection between the story of the patient's sufferings and the symptoms of his illness – a connection for which we still search in vain in the biographies of other psychoses.

Freud not only announces the birth of the modern clinical case history, he offers a theory of its literary form, a form that turns out to be involuntary, the effect of a kind of possession on his part by the hysteric's speech. He tells us that his training encouraged him towards the isolation and diagnosis of the hysterical symptom, and thereby towards the submission of the hysterical patient to the rigorous clinical and conceptual discipline of the doctor. And yet in the end it is the doctor who must submit to hysteria. The cases seem unnervingly to dictate their own form, indifferent to *any preference* of Freud's own, and as such render themselves strange even to their own author. The hysterical symptom simply remains mute in the face of those who would know it as a determinate, observable datum, electrical or otherwise. Doesn't Emmy say as much when, in response to Freud's question as to why she doesn't know the origin of her stammer, she *violently and angrily* responds, *because I mayn't*? What she protests against is the reduction of her inner life to the dimensions of a bald answer. In asking where her stammer originates, Freud is raising the rather more monumental question of why she is who she is. There is, Emmy shows him, no instant answer to such a question. If he really wants to know, he will have to let her tell what she has to say.

Such free-form speaking and listening, Freud implies, mock

the vaunted seriousness of science by coaxing it into association with literature, and so with the kind of airy imprecision science properly defines itself against. Most worryingly of all for the doctor's authority, it demands an immersion in the singular texture of the patient's inner life. The symptom yields its secret only by telling its own story.

Literature invades the scientific stage when the patient's story can no longer be reduced to a known quantity. Psychoanalysis is a way of attuning ourselves to this unknown quantity in you. It invites you to listen to, and at times be astonished by, what you say when you don't know what you're saying, to follow the track laid down by your own ignorance about yourself. It is, Bollas says, a means of discovering the polyphony and strangeness of the voice that's singularly yours. It introduces us to a self that's insuperably private and unfathomable, that can't be reduced to a quantifiable thing among things.

This is the meaning and force of psychoanalysis in a culture that increasingly manages our needs and desires by imagining us as so much data, whether genetic, neurological, social or economic. Psychoanalysis insists on a self that overspills the classifications to which science and consumer society would reduce us, a self that is fundamentally excessive. Psychoanalysis makes a claim for the value of the private life, where privacy is understood in terms of not what you do or own, but what you are. And what you are, it says, is double. Stories of doubles are compelling because they put you in contact with the possibility of an other in you, an internal stranger at once disturbingly unlike you and infinitely more like you than you want to acknowledge. Psychoanalysis is about your relationship to this stranger in you, the ways in which it drives and shapes your inner life and relationships.

★

In March 2011, the most chilling and traumatic of the proliferating stories of media intrusion emerged – the hacking of Milly Dowler's phone. The wave of public outrage following the discovery that journalists from the now defunct *News of the World* had accessed the missing, and later discovered murdered, girl's mobile phone messages introduced a new mood of self-reflection and ethical urgency into the public conversation around privacy, leading swiftly to the announcement of the Leveson Inquiry into the culture and ethics of the media.

Yet for all its moral self-evidence, there was and is something enigmatic in the visceral public outrage these revelations aroused. Why it is that intrusions into the private life of the dead, who are after all immune to them, should appear so much graver than intrusions into the private life of the living, who aren't? The public rage seemed to say that you can't casually lay hold of death and grief, as you might other dimensions of private life, as though they are so much tabloid fodder. Moral intuition tells you that there must be regions in another's experience that aren't yours to trample over. But why should it have been the victim of a brutal murder who made this imperative so immediate in a way that living victims evidently couldn't?

Where a victim of hacking is alive, the intrusion will always be perceived as partial. The hacker, it seems, wants to get at specific details, the concealed secrets of an individual's sexual or financial or political life. Whereas to hack into the lives of the dead, even when the manifest purpose is to obtain individual facts, implies a violation of the self as such, an offence against its very being. It needed a murder victim to show us that a living self exceeds the sum of its knowable parts. The taking of a life reveals a dimension of the self beyond the reach of any power. The outcry provoked by the Milly Dowler hacking intuits an impassable limit on your knowledge of the other, of an obscure spot in her that will and must remain in the dark.

The phrase 'the private life' is among other things the title of one of Henry James's lesser-known stories, which tells of the vain quest to see that obscure spot, to penetrate into another's inner darkness. The story centres on a motley group of bohemians and aristocrats holidaying in an Alpine village. Its unnamed male narrator and his actress friend, Blanche Adney, stumble during the course of their walks upon the bizarre secret of two of their party. The first is an aristocrat, Lord Mellifont, famed for the perfection of his speech, dress and manners – in other words, for the seamless exterior he presents to the world. The second is Clare Vawdrey, a renowned playwright whom Blanche is assiduously seeking to coax into writing a major role for her. What the narrator first discovers, and Blanche eventually confirms, is that away from the gaze of others, Mellifont simply evaporates. His purely public existence is annihilated as soon as he enters an empty room. But if Mellifont is merely half a self, Vawdrey, the story's denouement reveals, is double. The socially inept Vawdrey seen by the holidaying party secretes a second self, the real writer of his plays, in the privacy of his darkened room.

The story seems to say that the self is at once split (Vawdrey) and incomplete (Mellifont), both more and less than itself. Mellifont can be so entirely and effortlessly himself only by eliminating his private self, and with it any internal friction or conflict. James surely anticipates here the fantasy that governs today's culture of celebrity, the demand that they be no more nor less than they appear, that they withhold or conceal nothing, and so enforce the comforting ideal of a self that is integral and complete. As Mellifont shows, however, the paradox of this ideal self is that he can appear to add up to himself only by being less than himself – just as Vawdrey can perform the supremely private act of creating a work of art only by exceeding himself.

The narrator finds Vawdrey *writing at his table **in the dark***. James's emphasis on those last three words hints at a creative life issuing from a place that is fundamentally obscure. In the creative act, the self that speaks is a nocturnal self at once intimately known and radically strange to the familiar daylight self. The double writing at Vawdrey's desk, says the narrator, *looked like the author of Vawdrey's admirable works. It looked infinitely more like him than our friend does himself.*

Perhaps the narrator is speaking here not only of Vawdrey's double, but of the peculiar power of the work of art, its capacity to reflect the world back to us in a form both estranged and profoundly familiar. *There is another world*, says the Surrealist poet Paul Eluard, *but it is in this one.* It may be that Freud was getting at something like this when he found his medical case histories read unnervingly like works of literature. Yet he could also console himself that *the nature of the subject is evidently responsible for this, rather than any preference of my own.* There is something very telling about this apologia, with its implication that literary form provides not merely a more absorbing but a more rigorous representation of the patient's inner experience than the diagnostic classifications of psychiatry, above all because it encompasses the private life that classifying disciplines prefer to ignore.

Dream, poetry, analysis: exact sciences, runs the at once ironic and serious aphorism of French psychoanalyst Jean-Bertrand Pontalis. Psychoanalysis and poetry are exact sciences precisely because they eschew the definitive answers demanded by so-called hard science to questions of who and why we are who we are, showing us instead the experience of being a self in all its inconsistency, strangeness and duplicity.

Dream, poetry, analysis: three modes of creative life each rooted in a double residing in the dark, each trying to listen to that double tell what it has to say in its own obscure, nocturnal language rather than in the familiar generalities of waking life. Not that this language is any different from the everyday one spoken by you and me. The kinds of phrases that pass in and out of your mind or mouth in daily life – 'sick of all these shows about baking' or 'you can never find a hole-puncher when you need one' – could as easily find a place in a dream, poem or analytic session as in an ordinary conversation. But what they'd bring to the surface is a strangeness buried in ordinary thought and language, an eerie otherness that daily speech conceals. What this strangeness makes audible isn't simply the presence of the unconscious, but the singularity of the human person. Phrases wrenched out of context sound funny partly because they're divested of their generality, attesting instead to the stubborn particularity of the speaker, to what makes her irreducibly different from, even and especially when she seems to have so much in common with, everyone else. Vawdrey writes in the dark because it's the dark that protects and nurtures this singularity, that defends the self from sinking into the anonymous light of publicity.

The great French writer Maurice Blanchot suggests, in an essay with the ironically grandiose title of 'Humankind', that the most essential and elusive region of the self is one *no power . . . will be able to reach*. Writing of Robert Antelme's harrowing and beautiful concentration camp memoir, *The Human Species*, he attests to the many ways in which one human being can dominate, violate and crush the body and soul of another. And yet what finally humiliates the destroyer and drives him to his most enraged and depraved excesses is the unbearable knowledge that there's something in his victim he won't and can't reach, that eludes even the coldest and cruellest master.

The private life explored in the pages that follow has something to do with this at once most vulnerable and indestructible region of your self. Privacy is subject to unrelenting attack, direct and indirect, gross and subtle, precisely because it guards the strangeness in you that *no power will be able to reach*, that no amount of intrusion from science or media or state or friends and neighbours can render visible. All the light of the sun and stars can't alter the fact that you remain in the dark, private in spite of yourself or anyone else. That alone is what makes it possible to live in the light, to have a face you show to the world.

2

'Everything is public'

A party. Sluggish with a half-glass of white wine, I'm talking to a woman I don't know. Or more accurately, I'm nodding in rhythm with whatever it is she's saying, in the hope it'll distract from the vacancy of my stare. Most of her words dissolve into the hum of overlapping voices, leaving me with an insoluble rebus of verbal scraps. 'Funny . . . degree . . . jazz . . . Tiverton . . . irrelevant . . . Jesus'. Feeling a mounting pressure from myself as much as her to confirm I'm actually present, I hear myself say, with some doubt as to its relevance, 'I'm a psychoanalyst.' A sudden wordless squeal, pitched somewhere between hilarity and terror, jolts me out of my stupor as I'm caught in her startled accusatory stare.

Psychoanalyst. Something about the word provokes that kind of response. No sooner do I say it than I see myself reflected in the eye of my panicked interlocutor, shrouded in a sulphurous fog. I'm confronted once again with another's conviction that the psychoanalyst knows, that I have immediate access to the most obscurely concealed regions of the other, that I can take possession of secrets about her that even she doesn't know.

'I'm staying away from you!' she says as her reflexive horror subsides. 'No really,' she continues, seeming to take the inanity of my smile for wryness, 'you'd have a fucking field day with me. God knows what you're already thinking.' Having been so brazenly inattentive, there's a nice irony to being described as all-seeing. But then, whoever I am is no longer being seen at all. I've been swallowed up in the fantasy, at once creepy and seductive, that I pitch my tent in the innermost privacy of others. Suddenly she's under siege from both my voracious wish to know and her mad itch to tell.

In any case, the response breaks a spell. For one thing, she becomes fully audible, enabling me to discover that not all her associations to the word are negative. 'Psychoanalyst' also connotes intellectual seriousness, emotional intelligence, patience, a capacity to open up another person's curiosity about themselves. And yet we've both heard the squeal and its intimation of a sinister double lurking inside my apparently trustworthy professional exterior – a prurient, perhaps malevolent intruder into the other's heart and mind. It feels like my new acquaintance is having a conversation with both these men, the one characterized by his benign interest in a generalized mind, the other by his predatory readiness to raid the darkest corners of her inner life, to drag its most vulnerable and most protected contents into the lurid light of day.

Curiously, I've only rarely heard this fantasy voiced so explicitly in the consulting room. It's in casual social encounters like this, where the protective boundaries of the consulting room are lacking, that I find myself more liable to be confused with this pseudo-mythic figure endowed with the power to shine a kind of psychic ultraviolet into the other, causing the hidden interior of her soul to fluoresce shamelessly, like a naked body suddenly visible through its clothing. It's a moral and spiritual body under threat of exposure here, though, an essential badness she hears herself charged with as soon as I say that word. No wonder she's swearing to stay away from me.

The ambiguous pleasure of meeting someone new at a party is that you can show them as much or as little of yourself, in as candid or fictitious a version as you like. But when that someone is revealed as a psychoanalyst, the game is both spoiled and enhanced by the tantalizing possibility of being seen through. What will he see? What will you hide? Will the gap between who you are and who you say you are be kept intact or fatally exposed?

Alongside this threat of being seen for who you really are lies its more subtle mirror image, the threat of being confused with who you appear to be – an anxiety captured beautifully in a very short story by Lydia Davis:

What She Knew

People did not know what she knew, that she was not really a woman but a man, often a fat man, but more often, probably, an old man. The fact that she was an old man made it hard for her to be a young woman. It was hard for her to talk to a young man, for instance, though the young man was clearly interested in her. She had to ask herself, Why is this young man flirting with this old man?

Through the prism of this strange encounter, we glimpse what we're prone either to forget too easily or remember too self-consciously – simply put, that our inner and outer selves don't coincide, that what we show the other is more disguise than disclosure, even if we'd prefer it to be otherwise. The 'she' of Davis's story inverts the anxiety of my party acquaintance. Where the latter shrank from the horror of my seeing what she concealed, Davis's 'she' doesn't want the flirtatious young man to confuse what he sees with who she is. 'She' renounces the very protection of appearances my new acquaintance is in horror of losing.

Davis seems to be hinting at the unnoticed strangeness of being in the presence of someone else. You know who you are, and it seems as though all you have to do is convey that knowledge to the other person. But once you start talking, or remain silent or offer some expression or gesture, what you know – say that you're a fat old man – fails to match up with what the other person perceives. You have language, verbal and non-verbal, to externalize your inner self, but that language, instead of conveying intact your version of who you are, turns you against your will into someone else, perhaps someone entirely other than you know yourself to be. Your most private self resists the best efforts, your own included, to bring it to light. It's not just poetry that's lost in translation. It's you, too.

On the other hand, this picture of the private self as an internal alien hardly tallies with the popular notions of inner life circulating in our culture. We seem, on the contrary, to be living in an age of unprecedented intimacy with our private selves. Newspapers, magazines and the airwaves feed us with the varied entertainments of depression, marital breakdown, addiction, eating disorders, perversion and paranoia. The once specialized vocabularies of psychiatry, psychotherapy and psychopharmacology have been absorbed into everyday speech. Lifestyle sections, advice columns and chat shows extol the virtues of emotional openness. Hitherto unknown individuals invent their own celebrity by submitting their 'real' private lives to the compulsive scrutiny of the TV audience. Social networking has created the conditions for the permanent broadcast of our internal and external lives. Meanwhile, increasingly mindful of the virtues of mental and emotional well-being in an economy that loses billions of pounds each year to depression and other forms of mental illness, corporations hire 'coaches' to help their executives get in touch with their feelings. These economic risks haven't been lost on the state, which in this and other Western countries has been investing heavily in the promotion of a happiness agenda, spotting in the well-being of the labour force one potential remedy for the remorseless decline in the West's economic productivity.

Never, it would seem, has public culture in all its forms made such a priority of the care and cultivation of the inner self. Private life seems to have moved out of its repressed dark and into its liberated golden age. Only here you stumble on a basic contradiction. A golden age is a long moment in the sun, radiating its glories to all. It may be that such prolonged and intense exposure to the light has blinded us to the obvious point: placed in the sun, the private is no longer private.

Is the inner self nurtured or destroyed by our zeal to open it up to the gaze of the world? The question brings to mind the opening of one of the most powerful and prescient stories of private life and its exposure, *The Scarlet Letter*. Hawthorne begins his celebrated romance with the public disgrace of Hester Prynne in the marketplace of Puritan Boston, for bearing a child adulterously. Ushering her on to the scaffold and calling on her to show the assembled crowd the embroidered scarlet *A* on the front of her dress, the beadle proclaims *the righteous Colony of Massachusetts, where iniquity is dragged out into the sunshine.* Holding her baby, the shaming evidence of this iniquity, Hester is forced to bear *the heavy weight of a thousand unrelenting eyes, all fastened upon her, and concentred at her bosom.*

The light of a thousand eyes, and of the sun itself, is the Puritan remedy for sin. But Hester's public display doesn't end in the triumph of Boston's pious light over her corrupted darkness.

On the contrary, Hawthorne notes, in the face of her lush beauty, *the world was only the darker*. Her inner self is simply rendered more obscure by the effort to unmask it. For all the penetrative force of its thousand eyes, for all its concentrated focus on her heart, the crowd can't see what it's looking for.

Just how far is the profane glare of today's TV cameras and telephoto lenses from the pious light of Hawthorne's Puritan crowd? Don't they share the same zeal to purge the self of its secrets, the same hatred of the self's dark recesses? Whether in the guise of Oprah or the *News of the World*, the good cop who encourages you to share the contents of your inner life or the bad one who forcibly exposes them, our culture is as heavily policed as Puritan Boston's by beadles dragging our iniquity into the sunshine. And now as then, the fantasy driving all this frenzied looking is that with a sufficient glut of light, nothing will remain unknown to us. Nothing of others, and so finally nothing of yourself, will be left in the dark.

The problem is that privacy suffers the same inexorable fate when exposed as an undeveloped celluloid film. This, Hannah Arendt tells us, was a truth much more readily recognized by the ancient world. The Greeks, and the Romans even more, saw that light becomes an instrument of terror when it's allowed to rule without restraint. The integrity and meaningfulness of human life depended on keeping public and private rigorously distinct. This distinction, writes Arendt, *equals the distinction between things that should be shown and things that should be hidden*.

The best life for the Romans, argues Arendt, was a visibly active, public one. There was no higher aspiration than the citizen's free exercise of his mind and body in the service of the common good. But a virtuous public life of this kind wasn't possible without a private realm into which that mind and body could withdraw. The free Roman citizen experienced his daily venture into public life as a kind of crossing into light from the dark. That darkness, the place of elemental bodily need and desire, of birth, sex and death, *must be hidden from the public realm*, writes Arendt, *because it harbours the things hidden from human eyes and impenetrable to human knowledge*. For the Roman citizen, it wasn't simply a matter of there being more to you than the world sees – without this gap between what can and can't be seen, life would fall into chaos. Precisely because they were kept distinct, the citizen's private and public selves protected rather than competed with one another.

We moderns no longer submit to this darkness. If it persists, we flood it with sunshine of one kind or another. Birth, sex and death are abundantly accessible in the instant of a single google. *Privacy*, after all, as the tabloid journalist Paul McMullan told the Leveson Inquiry in November 2011, niftily encapsulating the spirit of a culture, *is for paedos. Fundamentally*, he elaborated, echoing uncannily his Puritan predecessors, *no one else needs it. Privacy is evil . . . it brings out hypocrisy*.

Hypocrisy is the essential iniquity for our tabloid culture as it was for the Puritan clergy. For the tabloid imagination, to afford private life this protection is *evil*, a nefarious cover for the most voracious criminal perversion. If there are *things hidden from human eyes*, it's imperative to wage war on them, to drag them on to the scaffold of global display.

There's an irony to celebrity culture having become the principal theatre of this war on hypocrisy – that is, on the concealed private self. For it was in the awed worship of celebrity that some small, distorted residue of the ancient division of public and private was preserved. That the stars of Hollywood's golden age might be someone else in private, that they might be concealing an existence that contradicted, complicated or deepened their glittering public persona, was precisely their allure. Yes, there were scandal sheets then, as there are anonymous blogs now, spreading whispers of addiction, adultery, homosexuality and other outrageous inversions of the lives on show. But such salacious gossip only polished the sheen of their enigma.

Whereas the self-invented celebrities of our own time have grasped the Warholian wisdom that their fortunes lie in cultivating not this celestial other-worldliness but rather their aggressive mundanity. Consider, in this regard, the following scene.

It's late. I've started from what I think was a brief but deep sleep, slumped on the sofa, clammily grasping the remote, the TV beaming some grainy rock video. Like Beckett's tramps, I keep resolving to go and not moving. I find myself surrendering to the self-hating inertia peculiar to late-night TV. My thumb presses absently on the channel changer. A steaming Malay beef laksa, Alice from *The Brady Bunch*, the stiffly choreographed rutting of a couple whose painstakingly sculpted upper bodies fail to distract from his missing penis, Australian Rules Football, the liberation of Belsen, Lembit Opik, Bod, an Irish shopping-channel presenter holding a glue gun in front of his face as he shouts the word 'nothing', Mr T: the images flash past in a catastrophic pile-up before my forearm crashes to the sofa cushion in weary defeat. I've stopped, with less arbitrariness than I'm willing to admit, at *What Katie Did Next*, and am enjoying the shame of my unwitnessed curiosity.

But it's not as much fun as I'd hoped. I find myself asking, less in the spirit of disdainful judgement than of genuine cognitive confusion, what it is I'm watching here. I'm seized for a moment by a bodily memory of sitting alone, aged fourteen, in the worn seat of an old repertory cinema watching Fellini's *Juliet of the Spirits*, anxious to prove a point I wasn't really sure of, feeling the chastening disappointment at my own incomprehension mount by the second. Then as now, it's not clear to me what I'm meant to be looking at, what this eerily disjunctive stream of words and pictures actually wants from me. The programme is cutting between a stocky orange-skinned man holding fancy-dress costumes up to a camera and the protagonist herself driving a Jeep, standing in front of horses, sitting on top of horses, kneeling down to her small children, sitting round a desk with some other people. Her sentences often tail off before they've had the chance to begin, leaving me with the sense of an unnameable sadness lurking in her permanent half-smile.

As the camera chases Katie running down a snow-covered drive, I suddenly feel like the nameless narrator of 'The Man of the Crowd', my favourite Poe story. A man sits people-watching in a London coffee house, enjoying by turns the smoke-wreathed company within and the streaming crowd outside. His gaze alights on a *decrepit old man* whose unreadable expression provokes a fascination so intense he resolves to follow him wherever he goes. The trail becomes more maddeningly and incomprehensibly aimless the longer he follows it, a frenzied sequence of false starts, blind alleys and tortuous circles. *I was at a loss*, he says, *to comprehend the waywardness of his actions*. He tails him into the following dawn, day and a second night, when the trail finally ends, exactly where it began. The old man resumes his *solemn walk* as the narrator ceases his in weary defeat. *'This old man,' I told myself, 'is the type and the genius of deep crime. He refuses to be alone.* He is the man of the crowd. *It will be in vain to follow; for I shall learn no more of him, nor of his deeds.'*

Thus too ends my near-hallucinatory forty minutes with Katie Price, an unfathomable wandering at the borders of boredom and compulsion. I say to myself, a bit too pleased with the melancholy paradox, 'The less you conceal, the stranger you become.' I've followed and followed, run haplessly at her back in desperate anticipation of what she'll do next, before it dawns on me that the more I follow, the less I'll discover. She doesn't do anything now, she only does things next. She's one long post-ponement – to follow her is to be condemned to a future that will never come. It will be in vain to follow; for I shall learn no more of her, nor of her deeds.

Much as I might join in the lament that Katie Price or Peter Andre do nothing, are omnipresent in spite or rather because of their lack of any discernible talent or interest, their fascination, and the compulsive hunger they exploit for the minutiae of their lives, lie precisely in this absence of any particular focus for your attention. You crawl down the burrows dug into their lives (with their unfailing cooperation) by the media, as though trying to discover what it is you want to know about them, as though you might somehow miss it, while the constant, indigestible drip-feed of dubious revelations tantalizes, without ever gratifying, the wish to know all.

Hawthorne's thousand-eyed crowd may have swelled into the millions, but it still suffers the same predicament: the more it sees, the less it really knows what it's looking at. Where celebrity once relied on the withdrawal of the star into an inaccessible darkness, it now lives off a flood of light which, in exposing everything, obscures your sense of what it is you want to see.

Lydia Davis's miniature story suddenly starts to read like an oblique commentary on this flood of light. Other human beings, it hints, are always obscure, however clearly we may think we see them. It's no coincidence that Davis's story reminds me of an essay by Maurice Blanchot gnomically titled 'Literature and the Right to Death'. No coincidence because 'What She Knew' is a kind of jocose eight-line condensation of Blanchot's dense, rambling forty-four-page masterpiece, which she in fact translated, meaning that for the English reader of the essay, his singular voice comes to us only through hers.

But Blanchot resonates here for other reasons, not least that this most revered and enigmatic of modern French thinkers and writers lived one of the twentieth century's most determinedly private lives. Born in 1907, he wrote and published prolifically across seven decades from the silence and anonymity of a Parisian attic. After 1945, dogged by ill health, he became increasingly isolated, refusing interviews and communicating with his close friends largely through correspondence, until his death in 2003. There are very few known photographs of him.

These sparse biographical facts might be incidental if they didn't echo so precisely the themes and motifs of his different bodies of writing: his unclassifiable, disturbing fictions and his matchless commentaries on other writers past and con-temporary. Blanchot's writings mine the great events of history and literature not for what can be known about them, but for what can't. He guides us again and again towards those regions of human experience which defy your attempts to understand them, as illustrated in the myth, which he repeatedly visits, of Orpheus.

Orpheus travels to the underworld to recover his beloved Eurydice. Moved by his song, the gods of the underworld agree to return her to Orpheus and the world above. But just as they're emerging into daylight, Orpheus loses her for defying Hades's condition that he avert his gaze from her until they've both reached the upper world.

Orpheus, suggests Blanchot, can't resist looking back because there's something about this nocturnal Eurydice of the underworld that will be lost to him in the daylight of the upper world. He wants to see the elusive dimension of her that can't be seen. He *wants to see her*, Blanchot writes, *not when she is visible, but when she is invisible, and not as the intimacy of a familiar life, but as the foreignness of what excludes all intimacy.*

If these words seem as strange and impenetrable as the experience they're trying to describe, so they should. Blanchot's writings begin at the moment where the contours of the known world dissolve, where what was reassuring and familiar is suddenly revealed as obscure and impenetrable. They concern that strange force within you that can't be perceived or communicated, like the 'fat old man' secreted invisibly inside the 'she' of Davis's story. Or like the secret self of my fellow partygoer, who recoiled in horror at the very possibility of being seen.

In 'Literature and the Right to Death', Blanchot asks why this private and inaccessible self is viewed with such suspicion by political activists, especially those intent on the revolutionary transformation of society. This isn't a matter of idle curiosity. Modern history, emphatically not excluding the moment at which I'm writing this, is littered with the mass graves of those deemed to have been keeping too much to themselves.

The exhilaration and terror of the French Revolutionary Terror, Blanchot says, is that it instated its own cause as the sole and universal one. Anyone who spoke or acted for anything or anyone else condemned himself at a stroke to death. *No one*, writes Blanchot, *has a right to a private life any longer, everything is public, and the most guilty person is the suspect – the person who has a secret, who keeps a thought, an intimacy to himself. And in the end no one has a right to his life any longer, to his actually separate and physically distinct existence. This is the meaning of the Reign of Terror.*

The Revolution, in other words, claimed a monopoly on all thought and action. Once this claim was established, everyone had a choice: surrender your private life to the Revolution and live, or hold on to it and be killed. Killing under such conditions becomes a chillingly empty act, *with no more significance*, in Hegel's terrible phrase, *than cutting off a head of cabbage*. The victim of such a killing, in *his actually separate and physically distinct existence*, is effectively already dead. The Revolution suffered you to live only as an expression and servant of its own interests. Life had legitimacy only when lived within the terms it dictated. Live outside those terms and you'd no more rights than a cabbage.

Private life provokes tyranny for the simple reason that it suggests the existence of truths that tyrants can neither possess nor control. Another of the twentieth century's great essayists and thinkers, Walter Benjamin, was forced to confront this reality directly. Benjamin's hesitant turn to Marxism was guided by his passionate and painful affair with a Latvian Bolshevik intellectual named Asja Lacis. In 1926, receiving word that she'd suffered a nervous breakdown, Benjamin left Berlin and followed her to Moscow, where he remained for two months. His intimate diaries of that period reveal the increasing tension, at times explosive, in his relationship with Lacis, whom he saw only during the daylight hours she was able to leave her sanatorium.

The peculiar irony of this episode is that Bolshevism had effectively outlawed the private passion which had driven him to Moscow. As Orlando Figes has shown, the Bolsheviks had identified private life at the outset as a danger to its very soul. *To allow 'a distinction between private life and public life', maintained Lenin's wife, Nadezhda Krupskaia, 'will lead sooner or later to the betrayal of Communism'*. Contracting to near zero the physical and social reach of private space, the breeding ground for counter-revolutionary thinking and acting, was one of Bolshevism's first imperatives. The effect of this policy didn't escape Benjamin's attention. In the essay on Moscow that came out of his visit, a series of sections celebrating the city's new vitality and dynamism is suddenly interrupted by his flat declaration that *Bolshevism has abolished private life. The bureaucracy, political activity, the press are so powerful that no time remains for interests that do not converge with them.*

Benjamin's bitterness had both a political and a personal resonance. He'd found himself at odds with the demand to surrender his intellectual and political independence to the will of the Party with which his lover was identified. His dilemma, specifically whether to advance himself by joining the Communist Party, expressed the more general dilemma whether to renounce the private life that had brought him to Moscow in the first place. He chose not to, cleaving instead to the position of 'left-wing outsider'. Benjamin was experiencing private life under the impossible conditions of its abolition.

Private life is the first enemy of totalitarianism because it harbours an otherness no amount of social control and surveillance can abate or control. Fascism and communism alike excoriated it, supposedly for distracting from the one true Cause, for its corrupting petit bourgeois triviality and irrelevance, but more plausibly for its essentially subversive force. As Blanchot has it, *the everyday escapes. In this consists its strangeness – the familiar showing itself . . . in the guise of the astonishing.* Private life means, yes, the driving passions, the outer reaches of the inner life. But it equally means breakfast, family birthdays, the irritable knock on the occupied bathroom door, all that's too contemptibly ordinary to warrant notice, and which for that very reason *escapes*. And the totalitarian mind can't abide what escapes.

Puritan New England, the Reign of Terror, Soviet Russia: no repressive state can properly sustain itself if it allows to grow unchecked those spaces in which nothing much happens, and in which, for that very reason, something very dangerous – a new thought, feeling or desire – *can* happen. Perhaps the same is true for the more subtly terrorizing culture of Murdoch's Old England. *Destroy the garden of the individual. Build a united garden*, ran the slogan of the Khmer Rouge. *Privacy is for paedos. Fundamentally . . . privacy is evil*, declares Paul McMullan, affirming history's Marxian habit of repeating tragedy as farce.

H., a very tall, rather ungainly writer, invariably looks down from behind his rimless spectacles when I open the door. He lies down and says what's on his mind. His speech is hesitant, cautious, at times exaggeratedly formal. But the close atmosphere is relieved intermittently by evocations of his inner states, the vivid elegance of which remind me of his vocation. He tells of rejections, real and anticipated. He insists on foisting his love on a woman who has repeatedly told him, without cruelty or ambiguity, that she can't return it.

I'm not sure why I like H. so much. I often feel exhausted after he leaves, as though the limit of my attention has been put to the test. I catch myself drifting, losing the thread of his associations. But when I try to think about this drifting, it strikes me as a mirror held up to his. I can feel, somehow always too late to catch it happening, that he only appears to be talking to me, that he's entered some interior zone into which I've not been invited to follow. At these moments, it's as though I exist in his mind less as an intimate listener than as some anonymous reader who's picked up one of his books, as though it's really to himself he's speaking and I just happen to be there.

But where does he drift to? For long stretches, he seems very present. He speaks affectingly of his irremediable loneliness, of the myriad ways he sabotages his own wish to connect more deeply with others. He's sure he doesn't want to be this way, always fending off the real possibility of intimacy, and yet he can't allow himself to be any other way.

I start to notice a pattern in our sessions. For a while, he spins out an insightful meditation on his own condition. We arrive at some formulation or other about his fear of real human contact, which, I note with self-punishing irony, itself doesn't quite feel like real human contact. Then, at some point in the middle of the session, there's that moment of mutual drifting, a going of our separate ways, which ends with me snapping abruptly back into the room in guilty embarrassment.

I resolved one day to follow his train of thought and my responses to it more minutely, to identify just where I was being sent astray. I was puzzled to be tuning into an account of his contretemps with a friend over a perceived slight. The mellifluous flow of his self-analysis had given way to a faltering, disjointed sequence of muttered half-phrases, anxious pauses, an indiscriminate shuttling back and forth through the story that made following it near hopeless.

I wondered aloud if he was aware of how difficult he'd made it to hear the story he was telling me. He paused for what felt like longer than it probably was. I waited out the palpable discomfort as he shifted almost imperceptibly on the couch. 'It's humiliating,' he said. 'I can talk to you about how I'm feeling or what I'm thinking, but to start telling you the details of some petty argument . . . He said, I said, he said. Details are so . . . ridiculous.'

There's something strikingly counter-intuitive about this shame in the face of details. A session with someone else will more likely begin with a deluge of detail, bridging the days or hours that have separated them from me. I'm flooded with the matter of ordinary life, of domestic frustrations and workplace tensions, husbands and bosses, friends and girlfriends, visits to the cinema or pub, nights working late or home early, rivalries, jealousies and resentments perceived and unperceived, usually offered without manifest inhibition or anxiety. Hesitation and discomfort kick in only when we move from facts to interpretations, when we start to explore the unconscious associations, meanings and motivations buried in the chronicle of events.

But with H. this sequence undergoes a reversal. He experiences the everyday less as a place to hide than to hide from. He swims freely in the depths of his inner life, but flails in the shallows of everyday facts. These, as he says, are humiliating, ridiculous. Why? Perhaps because in them he's revealed to himself and to me to be a little too much like everyone else – envious, inconsistent, self-deceiving and desperate for the love and approval of others. In relating the details of his spat with his friend, the admired writer finds himself staring in a funhouse mirror, reflecting back some grotesque infantile self he can't bear to recognize as his own.

Here is one of the paradoxes of what we often call emotional development. You imagine adulthood as a progressive differentiation of your self from the child you once were. People who are bored by babies and children typically remark that after all they're all the same, that one burbles and shits and cries much like another. To be a child is to lack the dignity of being properly yourself. Whereas in adulthood your thinking, language and creative activity become more precise, more elaborate, more distinctly and singularly yours. This is the punishing ideal against which H. is measuring himself, the fully formed adult who has shed the cumbersome chrysalis of his child self. And yet it's when he speaks at this maximal distance from the child he still is that I experience H. as most troublingly *un*like himself – and more like, to recall a David Byrne song, an advert for his own pale imitation.

Coming into contact with the child he can no longer bear to be causes in H. a kind of internal shutdown, expressed in a withdrawal from my presence which, as I came to discover, was being immediately and unconsciously mimicked by my response. Perhaps what he's defending himself against in those moments is the force of that third and final blow against humanity's ideal self-image, that *the ego is not even master in its own house.* H. is in every sense of the term brought low by his petty jealousies and cravings. He becomes at once too familiar, as squalid and silly as the rest of us, and unsettlingly strange, an internal other to whom he can't give voice without stammering in shamed confusion.

Freud has a name for this paradoxical meeting of the familiar and the strange within you: the uncanny or *das Unheimlich*, literally 'the unhomely'. It's the unanticipated moment when the very place you felt most at home is suddenly revealed as un-recognizably alien. It can cast its shadow as much over the face in your mirror as over the faces of others. When H. sees himself in the grip of his infantile passions, squabbling with his friend, he sees both a contemptibly familiar child and an unrecognizable monster. It's from this double that he's trying desperately to escape.

The intrusion of your unconscious is often felt as a shaming reminder of your limited authority in the home you thought was your own. A slip of the tongue turns a casual word to your boss into an obscenity, a small child provokes an outburst of uncontained fury, a memorial service triggers a fit of the giggles. 'I'm sorry,' you might say when you've recovered yourself, 'I'm not myself.' In one way you're right: your self has parted company for a moment from your 'I' and done its own thing. And yet why is it precisely at the moment you insist you're not yourself that you feel exposed as *precisely* yourself, as though your most vulnerably private self is on display to the world? How can it be that not to be myself is also to be most myself?

Perhaps because you're more than one self. It's no accident

that Freud's first clinical suspicions of the unconscious emerged from the treatment of fin-de-siècle Vienna's female hysterics. As his case histories so vividly show us, these women lived under intense social and emotional pressure to conform to their own public personae – that is, to have just one self. The outward composure of their dress, manners and speech demanded an inward counterpart in the good order of their thoughts and feelings. Under such repressive conditions, passions were felt as internal outlaws, mortal threats to the coherence and stability of the self from some other self.

Take Elisabeth von R., who tells Freud of being ambushed, on seeing the distraught widower of her sister standing tearfully by her corpse, by the irrepressible thought that he's now free for Elisabeth herself to marry. The intrusion of sexual lust into the solemn space of mourning is no mere social transgression. Lust in this context is felt by Elisabeth as an inner danger that must be banished to the outer reaches of consciousness. Eventually her private passions will be converted into bodily symptoms, pains in her inner thigh that both hint at and are slyly dissociated from their sexual source, silencing the someone else within. Hysteria arises when the inner demand to add up to one, to ensure that the self within is consistent with the self without, meets with the overwhelming feeling of being double, profoundly and irremediably divided.

H. is no classical hysteric in the mould of Emmy or Elisabeth. He's not beset by inexplicable tics, physiological symptoms or phobias. But in his own way, he is as afflicted as Freud's women by the fear of his own strangeness to himself, by the fact of not being himself.

I was still an adolescent when I first encountered Freud, an overbearingly earnest undergraduate, usually the first among a crowd of hundreds to pile into the first-year lectures on Literary Theory. The lecture on Freud and Literature was methodical, efficient, unexceptional, but it didn't matter. A personal tutorial with the man himself, scented with the smoke of his pipe, could scarcely have put me in more of a spin. It wasn't so much the bullet-pointed content of the ideas that overwhelmed me as a certain spirit of thinking, rising luminously from the background of its grey exposition. Like everyone else, I'd been taught from the moment I was teachable that what wasn't good was bad, what wasn't true was false, what wasn't beautiful was ugly. But here was another version of things, a way of thinking I heard as not merely interesting but as a kind of secret personal message. It said that the most glaring differences are in a relation of profound intimacy rather than of opposition. The most sublime ideas and the most abject madness, the highest morality and the most dangerous criminality are within touching distance of one another. It was astonishing less for its novelty than for disclosing a knowledge that had been lurking in me already, albeit unnamed, even unnoticed. It brought alive the unnamed sense I'd always had of feeling more tinglingly in contact with my murderousness and greed at just those moments I was presenting myself to the world as kindly and generous, the sense of being double.

Isn't this entire, unending world constructed by the understanding out of incomprehensibility or chaos? In these few words from the German Romantic philosopher Friedrich Schlegel, appearing in 1800, exactly a century before Freud's masterpiece *The Interpretation of Dreams*, is concentrated the entire massive, lumbering edifice of psychoanalysis, as well as that spirit of adolescent wonder it still excites in me. There's no knowledge, says Schlegel, no understanding, no distinct fact that hasn't been wrested from a reservoir of incomprehensible chaos.

In fact, this is almost exactly how Freud would come to describe the emergence of the perceiving (and misperceiving), thinking (and unthinking), understanding (and misunderstanding) agent within us we call *I*. The *Ich* or *Ego* (as James Strachey's unnecessarily technical translation has it) is a small pocket of coherence formed gradually and precariously from the formless soup of passions and impulses Freud calls the *Es*, or *It* (Strachey's *Id*).

Freud is taken to task by his detractors on many different grounds. One of the most common is his conception of the human being as hostage to inhuman forces within, the drives of sex and death. This may be the version of psychoanalysis echoed in the panic of my fellow party guest: you're going to see the bad person I really am. Except psychoanalysis doesn't think you're 'really' anything. It finds your truth in your being always more than one, in excess of yourself, irreducible to anyone else. The you that resists your sexual and destructive wishes is no less real than the you that wishes them.

So Paul McMullan was right about one thing: *privacy . . . brings out hypocrisy*, or the fact of being double. Hence his neo-Puritan, pseudo-prophetic demand that the hypocrite must be exposed, *dragged out into the sunshine*. What if this demand for the cleansing sunshine of knowledge masks the anxiety that there are places in you that sunshine can't reach? Underpinning the crusade against hypocrisy is the fantasy of a world in which secrets are eliminated, in which you have the reassurance of being who you think you are. This fantasy also harbours anxious knowledge of its opposite, namely that hypocrisy is your very condition, that inner secrets are the necessary corollary of an outward face.

Hawthorne comes to mind once more, this time in an early short story, 'The Minister's Black Veil'. It tells of the effects of the unexplained decision of the Puritan minister Reverend

Hooper of Milford to conceal his face permanently with a piece of black crape. The veil has an immediate and disturbing effect on his congregants, each feeling that the minister's veiled eyes see straight into the *secret sin* they hide within. *Each member of the congregation . . . felt as if the preacher had crept upon them, behind his awful veil, and discovered the hoarded iniquity of deed or thought.*

Only at the deathbed climax of the story does the minister yield up the secret of the black veil to his congregants. *What*, he asks, *but the mystery which it obscurely typifies, has made this piece of crape so awful? When the friend shows his inmost heart to his friend; the lover to his best-beloved; when man does not vainly shrink from the eye of his Creator, loathsomely treasuring up the secret of his sin; then deem me a monster, for the symbol beneath which I have lived, and die! I look around me, and, lo! on every visage, a Black Veil!*

Don't we hear in Paul McMullan some weirdly garbled echo of Reverend Hooper's dying protest? *Fundamentally . . . privacy is evil.* And yet, as the Reverend sees with painful clarity, it's an evil that's undeniably yours. The black veil is *so awful* because it reveals a truth both intolerable and essential: that no amount of openness and honesty can make you fully known to others, or even to yourself. Hooper expresses loathing for the veil obscuring the private self, and yet the ultimate lesson of his sinister behavioural experiment is that you can't lift this veil, regardless of whether you'd like to. In so far as it is the source of both contact with and separation from others, the means by which you simultaneously reveal and conceal yourself, your face is inescapably hypocritical. I can't exist in public without betraying a simultaneous and separate existence in private.

Where the tabloid crusader sees hypocrisy in the form of a knowingly duplicitous self-presentation, the psychoanalyst is more interested in your unknowing internal duplicity. Perhaps the rage against the former protects us from the anxiety induced by the latter. Perhaps the incessant focus on gross and deliberate instances of hypocrisy has the unwitting function of reassuring us that the vice can be localized, as though the gap between the inward and outward selves were peculiar to the morally defective. Put more simply, perhaps conscious hate for the hypocrisy of others is unconscious fear of your own.

3

Not at Home

An ordinary spring day. I was standing, age seven, outside the front door of the family home at the end of a school day, staring dreamily into one of the little bay trees that flank the front door. The weather was so benignly neutral I could imagine its purpose, were I bothered to think about it at all, as being solely to protect my peace. I was one of those kids the outside world had to grossly intrude on before he noticed it was there.

It wasn't an internal attitude well suited to the rigours of a north London prep school, where awareness is always the highest value, rendering the day a long, low-level assault of questions and insults and footballs, each laced with venomous irony or open hostility or hopeful expectation, to none of which I had any answers. But there are redeeming moments like this one, when my perpetual vulnerability to surprise seemed to yield its own secret if ambiguous reward.

The sensible world around me, sheltered under the bright grey sky, is as changeless as ever. The roses continue to lean imploringly over the path, their heads the same faded peach as the paper in the guest toilet. The reassuringly still commerce of cars and pumps and attendants at the garage opposite, the dully warm yellow of the house brick, the fey mulberry trim of my school blazer – all the signs of my profane eternity are present and correct.

Only because the world around me remains so eerily consistent can I receive the revelation that suddenly arrives, unbidden by me, unnoticed by anyone else. This, I hear myself saying in whatever language a boy of seven has at a moment like this, is my head, my body, and therefore no one else's. These feelings and sensations, even this very thought, belong to a place closed to any and all others.

If the current contents of my head were more remarkable, if they harboured some secret, outlaw feeling of love or hate or desire, the experience would be less so. But it's not so much that I have a secret than that I *am* one, that I'm being suddenly revealed to myself as bottomless, boundless, teeming with terrors and joys and banalities accessible only to me. Of course I can try to share them by telling you about them. But that will only make more apparent what I can't share, how very little you can know about the psychic and fleshly reality that is my private life. And what's more, I realize, noticing some vaguely familiar older kid staring straight ahead as he walks past the front gate, what's more this is true for you, and for everyone else as well.

Nothing has changed. The peripheral blur of my reflection in the oval mirror will flash up and disappear with the brown hiss of the doormat under my foot. The domestic perfume of frying onions, the plaintive yelling and chinking crockery, the painstakingly amassed collection of curling fruit stickers on my wardrobe door all confirm the sameness of the world.

But this confirmation that nothing has changed is somehow also confirmation that everything has, imperceptibly yet totally, as though it's the very sameness of the world that brings out its difference. What ten minutes ago was a kind of paper knowledge, abstract and barely thought, is now etched into my insides: I, like everyone else, am alone with myself. You and I look at each other from across an unbridgeable divide.

Lamb chops, *Peanuts* pocket books, a hair wash. It's an evening like any other. Except for some reason I feel I could cry, though I don't.

Psychoanalysis is forever presenting us with experiences which, from the perspective of the observable world, are non-events. To borrow Walter Benjamin's remarks on Proust, psychoanalysis orbits around *the great passions, vices, insights that called on us; but we, the masters, were not at home*. Like Proust, it sees the substantial portion of your inner life as conducted in your absence. You can no more be a reliable witness to the workings of your unconscious than to the burglary committed while you're out for the evening.

Take dreams, the first and still-essential object of psychoanalytic interest and the subject of its foundational work, *The Interpretation of Dreams*. Freud tells us that dreams matter so much for the very reasons the enlightened modern typically thinks they don't. Where the disillusioned rationalist sees only contemptible scraps of psychic waste, Freud sees *the royal road to the unconscious*. Think of your own cavalier attitude to your dreams. You laugh at them, disparage their senselessness and, worse still, forget them. You have enough to worry about in your waking life without being distracted by the nonsense you conjure up in your sleep. This unimportance, says Freud with his customary contrariness, is your strongest clue to their importance.

And the paradox multiplies. Not only does he tell you that the dreams you unthinkingly forget are worth remembering, but that it's their most forgettable elements that are most worth remembering. What in a dream is *worth remembering* isn't, as in waking life, *only what is most important, but on the contrary what is most indifferent and insignificant as well.*

The real substance of your psychic landscape lies in the forgotten, the unnoticed, the barely registered details. A refrain runs through the various hours of my analytic day: 'I had this dream that's really bothering me, only I can't remember it.' I said it in my own analysis more times than I care to remember, so often that I'm liable to lose contact with its brazen madness. I remember nothing and yet this nothing is bothering me, I can't help feeling this nothing is what really matters. If you're looking for a summary formula of the logic of psychoanalysis, one that brings out both its disturbing irrationality and its equally disturbing rationality, you could do worse.

Nowhere does Freud test this formula more audaciously – some would say more fatally – than in his famous case history of a young Russian aristocrat named Sergei Pankejeff, the so-called Wolf Man. At the centre of this case are a dream and its interpretation, brought by the adult patient not from the previous night but from age four. The dream insistently resurfaces across the years of the analysis, refusing to loosen its grip on the minds of both analyst and patient. Both of them sense it holds the key to the infantile disturbance from which Pankejeff has never recovered.

The dream begins with the four-year-old Sergei lying on his bed at night. The window suddenly opens *of its own accord, and I was terrified to see that some white wolves were sitting on the big walnut tree in front of the window. There were six or seven of them . . . In great terror, evidently of being eaten up by the wolves, I screamed,* and woke up.

A long and labyrinthine probing into Pankejeff's associations, spread over endless sessions, eventually yields Freud's famously, notoriously ingenious interpretation. The dream is an almost impenetrably disguised representation of the *primal scene*. Baldly, this is the moment at which the child witnesses the sexual coupling of his parents, as little Sergei did, Freud infers, in the summer of his second year. But it refers less to the scene itself than to its interminable afterlife in his memory. Freud has the four-year-old Sergei seized by terror and excitement, as the scene he'd witnessed uncomprehendingly as a toddler from behind the bars of his cot comes back to him in various guises, from picture book illustrations to dreams and hallucinations.

There is no eureka moment for this child in recalling the scene, no merciful relief brought by understanding. On the contrary, following the logic of any trauma, the original scene returns perpetually only because it's so tormentingly senseless. You can be haunted only by the incomprehensible. As long as what you see seems more or less continuous with the texture of life as you've always understood it, you carry on undisturbed. When you call to mind the ordinarily contented or even the more neutrally familiar experiences of your life, you're likely to see nicely composed photographic images – a tanned young couple by a pool, the mutually absorbed laughter of siblings on a climbing frame. Images that show you something, that confirm the world was and is as you believed.

But what the little Wolf Man recalls from that sultry afternoon is of a different order, intruding into his inner landscape a black spot of incoherence. He can make out in it no recognizable object or picture. You could say that he sees a sexual coupling, but this rather stretches the sense of the word 'see'. The infant witness of the primal scene doesn't see the sexual act in the sense that an adult viewer sees it when, say, looking at a pornographic image. Pornography achieves its titillating and finally deflating effect by reducing sexual experience to its immediately visible surface.

The image of sex is imprinted on the inner eye of the infant Wolf Man in a way that can't be contained by the contours of a clear picture. In its terrible obscurity, the scene shatters the clarity and reliability of the world he knows. He simply can't contain its excess, and this is why it comes back to him with such malevolent insistence. Its contents overspill the boundaries of both self and world, as though they have no place in either objective history or subjective memory, within his mind or outside it.

Your first intuition of sex, Freud is telling (or reminding) you, isn't the discrete 'adult' pleasure hinted at in the consumerist fantasies of Ann Summers or *Fifty Shades*. It consists not of artfully choreographed exchanges of words and bodies, but of an unbound anarchy of violent intrusions and helpless submissions. The older child's dreams and phobias of marauding wolves and lions, gnashing and roaring gleefully at their prone victims, disguise his traumatic fantasies of sex as orgiastic cruelty. The parental couple's afternoon delight, seen through the filter of their child's unconscious life, is a castrated mother's helpless yielding to a triumphally punishing father.

It sounds mad. As he reveals his theory of the primal scene, Freud anticipates his reader's incredulous double take: *I am afraid it will be the point at which the reader's belief will abandon me.* It's a lovely understatement of the predicament he passes on, quite unresolved, to anyone who wants to write psychoanalytically. Who today still believes this stuff? Freud intuits that a child's terrorized and excited fantasy of sexual life induces less scepticism than utter repudiation, an urge to turn your back on the very thought of it.

In the moment he anticipates his reader abandoning him, Freud also implicitly acknowledges the choice she has. In *The Birth of Tragedy*, Nietzsche frames this choice in terms of the contrast between the gaze of the philosopher and of the artist. The philosopher's wish, most famously expressed in Plato's allegory of the cave dwellers, is to abandon the darkness of confusion, madness and ignorance for the light of knowledge. Having unveiled the garments of the goddess Truth, the philosopher turns away from her concealed body, *takes delight in the cast garments and finds his highest satisfaction in the unveiling process itself.* Whereas the artist, writes Nietzsche, *remains with his gaze fixed on what is still hidden.* Perhaps this is where art and psychoanalysis have their deepest affinity – in choosing to stay with rather than abandon the darkness, to maintain contact with the obscured gaze of the child rather than retreat into the pseudo-security of the adult's enlightened vision.

But what does it mean to stay with the darkness? Not, to be sure, a gratuitous immersion in some hermetic retreat, internal or external, where you can neither find nor be found by anyone else. Not a space distinct from your familiar daylight world, but a foreign presence that's intruded imperceptibly into it. This is the darkness of Freud's uncanny, famously defined by him, via Schelling, as that which *ought to have remained secret and hidden but has come to light.* The uncanny secret as Freud defines it hides not behind but *in* the world you already know. Cast in the shadow of the uncanny, the carpets and book spines and cutlery and faces and ceiling cracks and voices that people your everyday life are rendered suddenly obscure. Not because they've been cleaned, or contorted or rearranged, but on the contrary because they're exactly the same as ever. Only a secret they always harboured, that might have *remained hidden,* has instead *come to light.*

Having taught psychoanalysis for many years, I'm repeatedly struck by how much more immediately and potently this notion seems to resonate than any other in the Freudian repertory. Almost everyone seems to recognize that moment when the most intimately known spot in your daily surroundings, the sight of a face (even the one in the mirror) or the sound of a voice or the touch of a surface, feels suddenly alien.

I can't help thinking here of *White Light/White Heat*, a 1975 performance piece by the American artist Chris Burden. Burden secreted himself on a high platform invisible from any point in the gallery and lay there for twenty-two days during which, he later explained, *I did not eat, talk or come down. I did not see anyone, and no one saw me.* Visitors entered an empty gallery in which there was nothing to see, hear or even anticipate. The sole content of their experience was their awareness of the artist's invisible presence above them. There was, Burden would remark, *something infuriating in the notion that a human presence was up there in the shadows under the ceiling, not speaking, not doing anything, just waiting.*

You imagine your eye, as you wander through this room, profoundly agitated not by the platform but by the room itself, and not by its difference but by its uncanny sameness. You're coaxed into perceiving some imperceptible layer of reality, not behind appearances but in them. The reality you've always and unquestioningly known is transformed even as it remains stubbornly unchanged.

Something strikingly similar befalls reality in the Wolf Man case history. The primal scene begins life as something like an objective historical event. Freud takes great pains to establish its occurrence, going so far as to locate it precisely in time and space. One late June afternoon at five, we're told, the waking infant Wolf Man opened his eyes to the sight of his parents in flagrante.

But twenty pages on, Freud inserts a parenthetical discussion of *the reality of 'primal scenes'*, casting doubt on the reliability of his reconstruction. Perhaps, he speculates, the scene wasn't real but unconsciously fantasized. Perhaps the source of the fantasy wasn't the infant Sergei's witnessing of human intercourse, but the four-year-old Sergei's witnessing of animal intercourse. He can't be sure either way: *I intend on this occasion to close the discussion of the reality of the primal scene with a* non liquet *['It is not clear'].*

So the primal scene can't quite be called real any longer, but neither can it quite be called imaginary. Having been pinpointed in time and space, it's now neither here nor there. *It is not clear.* With this disconcertingly candid admission of defeat, Freud launches us into new territory, a region of experience eerily suspended between existence and non-existence, a world that is and isn't your own world, as though your world as well as your self were haunted by its own double.

In 'The Uncanny', written just a year after the Wolf Man case history, this precarious reality becomes the defining feature of psychoanalysis itself: *I should not be surprised*, writes Freud, *to hear that psychoanalysis . . . has itself become uncanny to many people.* There's something quietly astonishing in this passing observation from a man who so proudly identified with the ideal of scientific rationality. Perhaps, it suggests, I haven't so much brought light to the dark as made the light darker. Perhaps the ambiguous gift I've bestowed on you is to show you *it is not clear.*

Looked at from one angle, then, the primal scene is nothing, and so changes nothing. The same parents continue to offer the same child the same smiles, embraces, sanctions, reproaches. And at the same time it changes everything, insinuating into the child's everyday emotional landscape an irremediable disturbance, which is only intensified by the possibility that it was all 'just' a dream or a fantasy or a hallucination. The familiar faces he knows so well are now haunted by the private faces he doesn't and can't know. The smile that once joined his mother to him now divides her from him. Nothing changes, and everything.

Perhaps this is why the phrase 'primal scene' comes to mind

with the memory of that spring day. Who knows what real or imagined sights, if any at all, fuelled that oddly tranquil moment of vertiginous insight in my seven-year-old self? It's only the outcome I have a clue about. I know that from that moment I could no longer think of myself as occupying a shared world. I could no longer trust that what I'm told or shown is all there is to what I hear or see, or even what I think I'm telling or showing others. This is the stage of childhood psychoanalytic developmental psychology calls *latency*. In latency, your voracious curiosity about your own and others' bodies is abruptly switched off, as your excited pleasure in their sensations and substances turns to disgust. It's the point at which, in other words, your infantile life migrates into the oblivion of the unconscious, where the secrets you'd been so intimate with recede into invisibility, only to resurface on the odd ordinary spring day.

'He's a secretive little bastard, that one,' I'll hear a man whisper of me a few years later, unaware, appositely enough, that I'm eavesdropping. I catch just barely the confusion of hostility and admiration in his tone, mirrored in the uncertainty of my own response. I feel reproached and yet vindicated. Thrown into a world dense with secretive big bastards, what else do you expect me to be?

I find myself toying with the dismaying possibility that Arendt, one of the most penetrating writers on the modern fate of private life, has it wrong where it most matters.

In *The Human Condition*, Arendt commends to us the ancient ideal of a strict division between public and private, *between things that should be shown and things which should be hidden*. Neither realm is properly meaningful, she says, without the other. For the Greeks, *a life spent in the privacy of 'one's own' (idiom), outside the world of the common, is 'idiotic' by definition*. On the other hand, *a life spent entirely in public, in the presence of others, becomes, as we would say, shallow.* Each will yield its own richness only if the separateness and integrity of the other are respected. Whereas modern life, on the contrary, has *introduced the utter extinction of the very difference between the private and public realms.*

Four decades after Arendt made this bold claim, the world fell into the ominous grip of the global *Big Brother* franchise. *Big Brother* invites you to submit to the sheer pleasure of this *utter extinction.* Appearing on UK TV screens in 2000 in a flurry of millennial hysteria, its initial fascination, at least for me, had less to do with the flirtations and squabbles, the breakdowns between and within the makeshift household, than with the broader drama concealed implicitly in all of these little dramas – the Arendtian spectacle of the dissolving boundary between public and private life. It's with only the mildest tinge of shame I recall my compulsive anticipation of the next instalment, which the increasingly preposterous banality of the content only enhanced.

The first series of *Big Brother* was for the most part stupefying, a Warholian exercise in disclosing the ultimate emptiness of speech and action. But what magnetized me (and perhaps you too) wasn't what might happen, but the simple fact of its happening. Every moment, however lacking in intrinsic interest, was enchanted by the dream of access to a private life other than my own. Here was the promised realization of Orpheus's deepest wish as imagined by Blanchot, to see the other person *not when she is visible, but when she is invisible.* Wasn't it just this fantasy that *Big Brother* tapped into? It would open a window not on the visible but on the invisible lives of others, the dimension of them you'd imagined was forever closed to you.

Later series became so dispiritingly boring because they lost the quality that had made it so interesting. Packing the house with needy exhibitionists, contriving all kinds of pseudo-scandalous couplings and conflicts, it pandered to an imagined wish to see more of the other *when she is visible*, confusing her private life with her dirty secrets. It generated drama and incident, those dimensions of life you can already get from novels, movies, even life itself. But in so doing it deprived itself of its only real source of meaning – the hope of encountering the *invisible* other, of burrowing into the obscure marrow of their everyday existence. If you watch the permanent stream of the house in the middle of the night, if you sit behind the anonymous eye of the camera and watch someone twitch and mumble in agitated sleep, their face hauntingly interchangeable in the infrared haze, if you catch yourself in the shame and pleasure of casually violating the other's invisibility, you can recover some sense of this programme's lost fascination.

Big Brother, parading the *utter extinction of the very difference between the private and public realm* as entertainment, is incontrovertible evidence of the rightness of Arendt's diagnosis of the modern malaise. But it also shows up its wrongness. For Arendt, it's neither the dark obscurity of the private nor the luminosity of the public that renders experience meaningful, but the movement from the one to the other. Appearance in the light is rendered meaningful only by its having emerged from the darkness.

There's a curious overlap in how Arendt, *Big Brother* and tabloid culture more generally conceive of private life as a *realm*, a region behind closed doors in which *things that should remain hidden* take place. This version of privacy as a realm of hidden rather than visible activity strikes me as oddly externalized, as though it consisted merely of the things you do that you wouldn't want others to see, or what we ordinarily call secrets.

If privacy is reducible to what you do when no one's looking, the intrusions of CCTV and the telephoto lens become oddly intelligible, even justifiable. Capture the drunken fumbling, the adulterous tryst or the furious row on camera, and you can have what you want, the very aperture into the invisible that eluded Orpheus. *Big Brother* roller-coastered into terminal, draining pointlessness by convincing itself, and perhaps even you, that your deepest fascination was for the secret dirty deed.

Freud and Blanchot suggest otherwise. What you really want to see is what's hiding in the light. The really impenetrable secret of the private life can't be protected by private security teams or ferocious PR machines. It can't, as Arendt seems to think, be circumscribed in space or time, because it is so palpably present in you everywhere, all the time. This is why Freud found he couldn't sustain the view of the primal scene as a specific event. The primal scene is less something that happens than the quietly devastating realization of a secret: those with whom you're most intimate, your parents and your own self, are also those who are strangest to you. This isn't a secret lurking in the dark. It's right there on the face across the breakfast table, in the mirror.

Perhaps this is what Reverend Hooper, the Puritan minister of Hawthorne's story, was getting at in his terrible deathbed pronouncement. You imagine, he seems to say, that this veil marks me out from you as hiding some terrible secret. But your face, for all its visibility, is no less concealed than mine. Your face is as much a black veil as this innocuous piece of crape – in fact more so, because the crape makes no pretence of being other than what it is. Unlike your face, it doesn't deceive, doesn't use its show of openness as a cover for the feelings, motives and desires it keeps concealed. That, in fact, is why you hate it so much, because for all it obscures, you see in it a terrifyingly clear reflection of your secret, sinful self.

The reassuringly clear line of demarcation commended by Arendt, between public light and private darkness, dissolves in the shadow of Reverend Hooper's dying address. He sucks into a vortex of doubt any last vestige of trust in your ability to distinguish reality and appearance, truth and falsehood.

Listen to the speech of people under twenty-five and you pick up a peculiar echo of Reverend Hooper. Born into a perception of reality as an infinitely plastic creation of technology and the media, they see on every visage – of politics, of finance, of celebrity – a black veil of obfuscating bullshit. The telephoto lenses, the Twitter leaks, the viral scandals, even WikiLeaks are just extensions of their own eyes and ears, confirming what they already knew. Obviously he's gay, she's bulimic, there were no WMDs, the bankers are on the take, it's all a scam, a cover-up, a conspiracy, a joke.

They possess the minister's penetrating gaze drained of its punishing religious passion, as well as of the humility that comes with it. The minister knows that the veil makes it not only impossible to see him, but also very difficult for him to see – that he isn't exempt from the darkness into which he plunges everyone else. The only thing he sees more clearly than the others is how dimly they all see.

The knowing young citizen of today's networked culture is less likely to doubt his own perspicacity. He wouldn't be naïve enough to imagine the public façade of any individual or institution as anything but the thinnest of fictions, a veil more transparent than black. What is contemporary celebrity culture if not a permanent invitation to its consumers to see right through it? You know that the loving smile of the couple captured exclusively by *Hello!*'s misty lens is only a subtly angled adjustment to the gritted teeth of mutual contempt, that the accompanying tales of one-kneed proposals on the peaks of

Yosemite or the London Eye have been hastily knocked up in a cubicle of a melancholy self-loathing by a tired PR consultant. Point this out to a passing adolescent, a pre-teen will probably do, and they'll respond along the lines of 'Yeah, and d'you hear Father Christmas isn't real either?' Not only is it all patently fake, no one's bothering to pretend otherwise.

In Puritan Milford as today, the private reality betrays the public face. Only today, private reality lacks the obscurity the minister saw in it. The secrets raked up by tabloid culture have no more truth or substance than the empty public selves they unmask. The Nazi-themed S and M orgy, the cross-familial adulteries, the secret (or not) sex tapes flow into the same inexorable tide of disposable stories and images. Secrets no longer harbour any secrets.

Everything has been dragged into the light; you've seen it all. So why keep looking? Do you imagine the next story will be any more tantalizing or, ultimately, any less unsatisfying? Perhaps what fuels the compulsive consumption of revelations and confessions is the madly Orphic hope of burrowing through to the invisible substance of the other's private life, to the desires, needs, pain, cruelty and vulnerability that render them *someone else* even to themselves. This is what can only elude you, what you feel you've been cheated of whenever you read *Heat* magazine or watch *What Katie Did Next*. Revelations of dirty secrets don't bring their shamed or brazen holder to light so much as taunt you with how much they remain in the dark. Tabloid culture is one long, torturously repetitious failure to bring the night of private life into the day of public knowledge.

Peering along the shelves of a Boston bookstore thirteen years ago, I caught the name of Lydia Davis on the spine of a slim volume. It triggered the fuzzy memory of a casual exchange in the pub with my PhD supervisor. I'd been talking to him about a novel by Paul Auster. What interested me about it, I'd said, was how instead of building your knowledge of the characters and narrative, it somehow depleted it, leaving you knowing less when you finished than when you started it. *Nng*, he grunted, 'you should read his ex-wife', whose name fell more or less immediately into a hole in my memory, only to give me an inexplicable start as it flashed up again in Boston four years later. I prised the volume off the shelf with an urgency I couldn't account for, as though too much was at stake to risk leaving it for another day.

Why does a writer take hold of you and refuse to let go? How is it you start to experience their work not as an object of external interest, but as an insistently troubling internal companion? I often resent the books I love most, and not only because of the furious, desperate envy they arouse in me. Certain books behave curiously like a psychoanalyst, putting me in contact with my sorest points of vulnerability, anxiety and confusion. I read *Moby-Dick* or *The Trial* or *Emma* and they provoke the very thought I'd sometimes find myself trying and failing to fight off during my analysis: surely I'd be better off if I'd never started this. A similarly hopeless resistance is aroused by falling in love. Everything about the book or analyst or lover enriches your experience, deepens your passion and curiosity for your own and others' lives, your sense of involvement in the world. But this passion is as intrusive as it is enriching. It creeps insidiously under your skin and into your soul, leaving you with the feeling that whatever life might be ahead of you, it won't be quiet and untroubled.

Some books you find yourself less reading than being read by. They introduce you to private feelings and convictions you realize had been incubating in you, waiting quietly to be discovered. This is how I can best describe my experience of the first story in Davis's collection *Break It Down*, to which I turned as I sank into one of the cynically plush leather armchairs that sealed my ambivalent love of large American bookstores. It was called, is called, 'Story'. Had the story itself been archly self-conscious, I'd have ended up hating that title. But for all its quiet self-assurance, it seemed to me more bald than ironic.

It had the quality of a friend's weary report of the latest chapter in an affair you both know is doomed – the same sense of aimless brooding, of that half-apologetic, half-petulant style in which your friend, or you, will relate a non-event as though it meant something – stirring up the suspicion in you both that it's pretending to be a story in the melancholy knowledge that it really isn't.

I get home from work, it begins, *and there is a message from him: that he is not coming, that he is busy*. Somehow you know straight away that this is the story: an encounter that keeps failing to take place. He's said he'll *call again*, but he doesn't, so the narrator goes round to his place, *but he's not home*. She returns home, waits restlessly for his call, before deciding to call him *at ten-forty-five*. He's at least home at this point, but *he has been to the movies with his old girlfriend, and she's still there*. So he'll have to *call back*, and she'll have to resume waiting. She fills the time writing in her notebook *that when he calls me either he will then come to me, or he will not and then I will be angry, and so I will have either him or my own anger, and this might be all right, since anger is always a great comfort, as I found with my husband*.

I read these lines and shuffle uneasily at their raw candour, yielding to the illusion that I'm stealing a glance into the private record of the very thoughts she wouldn't want anyone else to read. Only very quickly it's as though it's my rather than her inner privacy that's been invaded, as though I'm the one who's been caught in the indignity of this subtly shameful thought, if

I don't have the one I love, I at least have my anger. Only it's not 'as though' I've been caught, I really have been caught. This story has turned me into the reluctant voyeur of my own private madness, has rubbed me up against the someone else that I am.

Finally, *a little after eleven-thirty*, he calls back. They argue aimlessly for half an hour until the exchange starts *to sound too much like too many I had with my husband*, at which point *I say goodbye and hang up*. She returns to her notebook to realize in dismay that *it no longer seems true that anger is any great comfort*. She calls back to apologize and tell him she loves him, *but there is no answer*. She tries again five minutes later, *but again there is no answer*.

In fact, the phrase *no answer* will have recurred four times in less than three pages, acquiring an increasingly disturbing resonance with each repetition. No answer to what?, you want to reply, as though the words are losing their mooring in the situation they describe and taking on the sense of a generalized existential lament: *There is no answer*. I survey the vast rectangular plane of the upper floor of the bookstore, punctuated everywhere by clearly labelled mahogany-effect bookcases bulging with titles, newly alive to the cacophonous proliferation of sub-genres as a pile-up of vain efforts to respond to this elemental cry of the soul. *Self-Help, Eastern Religion, New Age, Health and Beauty, Love and Sex, Money, Home Improvement.* There is no answer.

I'm faintly aware of feeling quite upset, by the story or the bookstore or both. I return to the page to find her speculating with poignant neediness as to whether he might have missed the call walking to his garage or study. It's past midnight by now, *and I have to leave the next morning at five*, but nonetheless *I get dressed and drive the mile or so to his place*. Seeing an unfamiliar car, she thinks the old girlfriend is there. She walks round the back of the building to peer into his apartment, where *the light is on, but I can't see anything clearly because of the half-closed venetian blinds and the steam on the glass.* She knocks. *No answer.* As she walks to his garage, he emerges from the apartment. But *I can't see him very well because it is dark in the narrow lane behind his door and he is wearing dark clothes and whatever light there is behind him.*

This, I hear myself thinking, my head smarting a little from the excessively tight knitting of my brow, is unbearable, unsure whether I'm referring to the narrator's experience or my own. Every frustration I've ever suffered, every wearing sequence of anger and defeated resignation seems to be concentrated in this image of her trying and failing to see what's in front of her. Nothing, I tell myself in solemn solidarity, is ever clear, not even, especially not, the things right in front of you.

As he puts his arms around her silently, she thinks to herself, *he is not speaking not because he is feeling so much but because he is preparing what he will say.* He lets go and she walks with him towards the garage, *waiting for him to say that she is here and also that it's all over between us,* only he doesn't. She feels nonetheless that this had been the intention but that *he then thought better of it for some reason.* Instead, he apologizes, takes responsibility for the mess the evening has become, and lets her know the old girlfriend hadn't been there when they'd spoken, and is there only because *something is troubling her and he is the only one she can talk to about it.* Then he says, 'You don't understand do you?'

It feels like it's me he's talking to, as though he's peered askance out of his own story to address this question to me, as though I'm the one struggling to see him in the obscurely lit midnight. I came in here with half an hour to kill, thought I'd read a story, even found one called 'Story', only now I feel like the half-hour and the day and perhaps everything is ruined, there is no answer, I don't understand.

But there's a coda, the night's afterlife. She broods, tries *to figure it out*. There is his version of events: he and the old girlfriend went to a movie, came back to his. She called, the old girlfriend left, he called back. When she called back there was no answer because *he had gone out to get a beer*. She then drove over, just as *he had returned from buying beer and she had also come back and she was in his room so we talked by the garage doors.* But can it really be that they both returned *in that short interval between my last phone call and my arrival at his place*? Perhaps instead she was waiting somewhere outside as they spoke, and *he brought her in again* when the call was over, subsequently leaving the phone to ring without answering, *because he was fed up with me and with arguing*? Or had she indeed left, so that it was him alone who *let the phone ring without answering. Or perhaps* she remained while he went out for beer and *listened to the phone ring*? That seems to her the least likely option. *I don't believe anyway that there was any trip out for beer.*

I get deeply involved in this conundrum, finding this careful analysis of the relative feasibility of each version of events an immense relief from the draining disappointment and humiliation of what has preceded. Although I'm sorry to suspect that her scepticism towards the final option may be an effort to fend off the thought of the worst. I'm not sure if I could bring myself to tell her I can just see her sitting there, the old girlfriend, staring at the ringing phone, smugly awaiting him and the beers.

The episode is an instance of the more general conundrum of how to work out if he's telling the truth given *that he does not tell me the truth all the time*. Sometimes she figures not, sometimes she doesn't know, and sometimes *I am convinced it is the truth because I don't believe he would repeat a lie so often.* Which is a neat but not altogether convincing way of clawing back a little clarity. Because the truth is, if you can still use that phrase, the truth is once you know someone doesn't tell you the truth all the time, you're stuck not knowing if they ever tell you the truth. And this is quite a discomfiting revelation once you ask yourself who, after all, tells the truth all the time.

She'd like nonetheless to know the truth, *if only so that I can come to some conclusions about such questions as: whether he is angry at me or not; if he is, then how angry; whether he still loves her or not; if he does, then how much; whether he loves me or not; how much; how capable he is of deceiving me in the act and after the act in the telling.*

And so this story of a non-event, the sort of story you might listen to with good-humoured impatience if a friend related it, turns out to have at stake nothing less than the possibility of truth itself. Non-events like this make it impossible to distinguish clearly between a concealed private life, confined behind closed doors, and a visible public life open to all. They show you how insidiously private life, in all its obscurity, intrudes itself into the texture of your supposedly shared, supposedly public world. Even as she tries to relate events with maximal plainness and economy, with a detective's indifference to all but the verifiable facts, she still finds herself unsure how much she's been deceived, both *in the act* and *in the telling*, as though the verifiable facts were just the black veil interposing between her and the truth.

This is now my position as I sink back into the chair, caught in this contagion of uncertainty. It might be that I too have been deceived *in the telling*, by him, but also by her, because this after all is just a story, just words on the page, occupying that same nether space between existence and non-existence as dreams. I look at people hovering in front of shelves, compelled by their concentrated deliberation before this indigestible glut of ideas and counsel and stories. They're in the public domain, these browsers, entirely visible to whoever wants to look and yet also somewhere impenetrably private, entirely invisible. You don't know, *they* don't know, what strange concatenation of needs and wishes and anxieties is drawing them to look at this or that book, what answers they're seeking, what question they're asking. If you're inclined to voyeurism, a bookstore is the best and worst place for you.

Non liquet ['It is not clear'].

I look around me, and lo! on every visage a Black Veil!

Reverend Hooper's lament raises the age-old conundrum of trust and whether it's possible. And his anguished answer is no. You can never eliminate the suspicion that the open face of a person or the truthful ring of a story is just a cover for what they're hiding. Hence his vision, from the height of his mortal piety, of a world in which *the friend shows his inmost heart to his friend; the lover to his best-beloved; when man does not vainly shrink from the eye of his Creator, loathsomely treasuring up the secret of his sin.*

I never fail to feel provoked by this speech, to the point where I want to slip into the scene and sit alongside the assembled crowd around his deathbed, abandoned with them to the damned world he's vindictively departing. It feels like we're being stripped by his words of the precious illusion that made it possible for us all to live with one another – that we could trust each other to be more or less who we seem to be. The provocation is intolerable – I have to speak out, even if I risk desecrating the scene.

'All right,' I begin, rising tentatively to my feet, my pilgrim's hat held solemnly across my middle, my voice betraying more trepidation than authority. I catch a glimpse of his weak chin as the veil angles towards me, blown upward by his rasping breath.

'All right, point taken. But Christ, Reverend, what do you want us to do? Granted, we probably all do conduct ourselves and our relationships under the colossal presumption that we know who we are, and who we're with, when even the most cursory inward glance assures us this can't possibly be true. No doubt we all breezily smile and chatter and flirt without even bothering to ask ourselves whether we might have got things wrong, whether we shouldn't be more cautious in the assurance and trust we glibly confer on ourselves and others, in speaking and acting and even thinking as though what we see on the other's face coincided with the whole truth, as though we could trust what we see. But, Reverend,' I continue, on an unstoppable roll now, 'what's the alternative? It's hardly ideal to reduce the infinity you are, that every self is, to the tiny fragment you exhibit on the surface, but what would life be like if we didn't? You want a world in which the friend shows his inmost heart to his friend? But why? What can the world, or this glum little corner of it, have done to you that you'd want to turn it into this vast enforced encounter group? Or is this some cosmically malignant prank of yours? As your soul ascends to the heights will it holler down to us poor saps, now stranded in this hell of mutual exposure, so long, suckers! What if, just what if, Reverend, I don't particularly want to show my friend my inmost heart, and he doesn't particularly want to see it? Has it even occurred to you, you spiteful old bastard, that once you show your inmost heart it's no longer inmost? Or that if you could see through the black veil of words and faces, you wouldn't need to trust them? The thing is, Reverend, if you knew you could trust someone just by looking at them, you wouldn't need to trust them. Ridiculous as it sounds, you can trust people only because you can mistrust them.'

Pause. 'OK.' I shrug, my animating ire drained away. 'I'm done. Sorry.'

I'm sure as I can be that through the duration of this spontaneous outburst his milky eye has been calmly boring into mine from behind the veil, that I can feel it on me, in me, now. No one moves or says a word, the darkening room an immobile tableau of impending death. Only I seem to have sparked the dying minister into one last, unbidden burst of life. Waving away the proffered aid, he gaspingly props himself on to his elbow, facing me all the while.

'You don't get it, do you?' he spits, with the gleeful contempt special to those with nothing left to lose. 'You think I'm enjoining you all to reveal your true heart? But why, then, did I insist my veil could never be removed while I remained alive, if not to show you that yours couldn't either? How else could my veil symbolize your face if it wasn't permanently riveted into place? You think I imagine that all you have to do is be open or be yourself or some such inanity and the people of the world will join hands and form a love train? What kind of Pollyanna-ish halfwit do you take me for? The only Pollyanna here, my friend, is you, you and the ridiculous future you come from. You're the ones who seem to believe the world divides reassuringly between what's behind and what's in front of the closed doors in your house, or your self, and all you have to do is sit on a sofa with your trusted confidante, preferably in the healing light of the television studio, and behold, the doors will open and the secrets will be no more. So try again to listen to me: *on every visage a black veil!* Don't you see? Your secrets aren't behind your face, they're in your face. The sordid little secrets you hide from others are trivial compared to those you hide from yourself, those obscurities that hide in plain sight. Just look, if you can bear to, and you'll see that my veiled face is no more opaque than your naked one. You'll see the entire world plunge into obscurity, even as it stays exactly the same. All I'm asking you to do is look.

'And now, if you don't mind, I'd like a little privacy.'

4

Mysterious Parts Concealed

A seminar, some years ago. Twelve of us are lining the walls of a cramped basement room. We've adjusted to the uncomfortable incline of the seat cushions, dislodged from the frames of their low chairs, seeping crumbs of yellow foam from their threadbare grey covers. The monstrous fungal growths dotted round the ceiling's edges, the January draughts blowing round our ankles through holes in the skirting, the curls and bubbles in the damp magnolia lining paper are met with the same resigned lethargy. These dank, uninhabitable townhouses, along with the tinny Portakabins behind the tennis courts, are the college's desperate solution to the problem of its ratio of students to rooms.

I'm pissed off about the assignation of my Freud and Love class to this musty pod of decay. My agitated mind swarms with fanciful speculations about its meaning. Is the room booker making some winking allusion to the cesspit of the Freudian unconscious, or to the abject status of psychoanalysis in our brave new era of neuroscience and behavioural therapy. Looking round this room, I feel as though I've stumbled into one of those painfully earnest 'inspired by a true story' movies starring Morgan Freeman as an oil surveyor turned book smuggler running a dangerous clandestine operation to supply a group of Burmese dissidents with the outlawed words of Jefferson, Lincoln and Dr King. Naturally he ends up dying of a military bullet to the heart, smiling beatifically, whispering with his last breath to the tearful disciple kneeling over him, 'My people seized their freedom – now it's your turn.'

It's not the most congenial setting for a discussion of the *Three Essays on the Theory of Sexuality*. No one sitting here can be much in contact with the imperative of pleasure. Worst irony of all, we're discussing a famous passage from the last of the *Three Essays*, an evocative, lyrically precise love scene between a mother and her baby. Glumly recalling the Book of Lamentations, I hold back a tasteless wisecrack about this being the kind of room more likely to witness a mother eating than kissing her baby.

I'm not sure how much if anything all this has to do with the turn the discussion takes. I'm explaining to my students Freud's idea of the baby at the breast as *the prototype of every relation of love*. Your mother initiates you into love's impenetrable secrets. In one way or another, your later erotic experiences will all reach back into these earliest ones. *The finding of an object is in fact a refinding of it*, writes Freud. I continue reading aloud: *A child's intercourse with anyone responsible for his care affords him an endless source of sexual excitation and satisfaction . . . This is especially so since the person in charge of him, who, after all, is as a rule his mother, herself regards him with feelings that are derived from her own sexual life: she strokes him, kisses him, rocks him and quite clearly treats him as a substitute for a complete sexual object.*

As I look up from my text, one student is staring fixedly into hers, disdainfully shaking her head. This is D., a few years older than the others, less embedded in the sealed-off social and intellectual enclave of graduate life. Put another way, she has other things to do than sit around all day rereading the same paragraph in front of rerun DIY shows (I speak from experience). She responds to what she reads and hears with a rare immediacy and conviction, uncorrupted by the anxiety and self-doubt which filters almost every utterance of her colleagues. For the most part this is intensely refreshing, even if her flat self-certainty can swiftly shade into irritating. Her stance often involves trumping the theoretical with the personal, and today is no exception.

She leaps into the pause. 'I'm sorry,' she says, not at all sorry, fixing me with an incredulous smile, 'but do you actually *believe* this?'

'You obviously don't . . .'

'No I bloody don't. I'm a mother.'

A pause as we take this in.

'OK,' I say. Then, with ill-advised disingenuousness, 'so . . .?'

'So? *So?* So I don't bloody *perv* on my kids, that's what's *so*.'

A younger man intervenes, tall, skinny, nice-looking, enthusiastic, well-meaning: 'But you, like, kiss your kids, yeah?'

She turns on him a look sufficiently withering to hint at the complete irrelevance, not only of his words, but of his being.

'Yes, Rob,' she says, pronouncing the words with the aggressive mock-benignity that sooner or later seeps into the voice of every new parent and primary school teacher. 'I kiss my kids. I didn't say I don't kiss my kids, I said I don't perv on my kids.'

'Yeah, no, I know,' he persists, his smile an avalanche of redundant goodwill. 'But, like, it's unconscious?'

'Oh, I'm sorry, I stand corrected. All right, I don't *unconsciously* perv on my kids. I don't consciously, unconsciously or semi-consciously perv – on – my – kids.'

A frosty silence descends on us for a moment, a Cagean amplification of the bad-tempered hoots and sirens of the passing traffic outside.

'Well, no, of course,' I wade in, now experiencing the room's chronic state of disrepair as a mocking reference to the entropy of my own seminar.

Is the real substance of D.'s complaint merely a resistance to the discomfiting intimacy Freud observes between motherhood and sexuality? It strikes me that what's more at issue is her right to knowledge and ownership of her own mind, to be the best judge of what she thinks and feels. It seems difficult, if not downright impudent, to argue with this claim.

The common social and legal sense of privacy would seem to support D. here. We claim the right to privacy, to protection against unwanted intrusion, as much for the mind as for the body or the home. Privacy is indelibly linked, from this perspective, with ownership or possession of my self and its property, material and intellectual. It implies that I know what is and isn't mine. Psychoanalysis doesn't deny the need for these external boundaries around the self, but it puts in question the claim implied by this common conception of privacy that you are master in your own house. There is, in other words, a region of yourself that even you can't enter freely, as private to yourself as to others, locked, alarmed, watched over by dangerous guard dogs of one kind or another.

Far from owning this dimension of your private self, or the unconscious, you're a stranger to it, and not always a very friendly one. It doesn't want to know you, and as it turns out, you don't want to know it either. In fact, Freud suggests counter-intuitively in his 1915 essay 'The Unconscious', you are a better reader of the inner lives of others than of your own. This seems odd inasmuch as you have no access to other's inner states, and so have to infer them on the basis of *their observable utterances and actions*. I can't taste the ice cream in your mouth or feel the hammer strike your fingernail. I get a sense of what you're feeling in these moments by reference to my own inner history of pleasure and pain.

But, Freud continues, there's a peculiar resistance in us to the psychoanalytic demand *that we should apply this process of inference to ourselves also.* You know exactly why your friends make such disastrous romantic choices, fail to make progress in their careers or can't stop biting their nails. So why are you so unwilling to see, let alone comprehend, your own irrationality?

To be human, it seems, is to lack self-awareness. Locked into your own consciousness, you aren't *constitutionally inclined,* says Freud, to treat yourself as another in this way, as though *some special hindrance . . . deflects our investigations from our own self and prevents our obtaining a true knowledge of it.* And yet true knowledge of yourself requires precisely this: *all the acts and manifestations which I notice in myself and do not know how to link up with the rest of my mental life must be judged as if they belonged to someone else: they are to be explained by a mental life ascribed to this other person.*

A strange and wonderful paradox: you can't know your true self unless you've recognized that it isn't yours at all, that your most deeply private self belongs to *someone else.*

D.'s point, surely, is that no one wants to be told they're *someone else,* that where they feel the deepest and most immediate conviction in who they are, they're actually deluded, and haven't a clue what they're thinking or feeling or doing. Who are you to tell me I don't know the difference between a baby and a lover? is her indignant riposte to Freud, and it should be taken seriously by psychoanalysts above all.

Psychoanalysts, myself included, can be too quick to assure the likes of D. that it's all a misunderstanding, that to ascribe to another person unconscious wishes and desires, however alien, destructive or perverse, is absolutely not to condemn them morally. You see, we seem to want to say, we're all the same! We all unconsciously confuse sex and affection! We all perv on our children! It's fine!

This standard psychoanalytic defence isn't exactly wrong. But in its zeal to reassure both itself and its detractors of its harmlessness, it misses the force and insight of the protest it's defending against. People don't hate psychoanalysis because they're prudish or close-minded, but because it penetrates to the self's core. Just to read Freud, D. implies, is to experience a profound invasion of privacy, to feel that someone's trying to revoke your rights over your head and heart.

And so I'm wary of rushing to show D. how much she's failed to understand, and so of passing over what she's understood all too well, perhaps more viscerally and authentically than the rest of us sitting round this godforsaken room nodding sagely at all the talk of incestuous wishes. What in hell is wrong with you people?, D. implicitly reproaches us. Do you not hear what this man is saying about you?

She has a point. Something in what he says falls outside our range of hearing. Not, admittedly, the grossly voluble accusation D. hears, that your parental tenderness is really disguised debauchery, but the imperceptible and much more disturbing whisper that somewhere in you, so private you're barely aware of it yourself, you don't yet know the difference. Somewhere in you, the distinctions between sex and affection, between one and another mode of loving – distinctions on which your sanity, perhaps the very sanity of the world itself, depends – have yet to be learned.

D. is right: if you don't experience a shudder of horror and disgust on hearing this, you haven't been listening. It's the sound of the solid world you know being sucked inexorably into a blind vortex where chaos reigns, where sex has no place of its own but is everywhere and nowhere, sowing mischief, confusion and terror, where the boundaries between one word and another, one experience and another, have dissolved. Here in this crumbling basement room, D. is doing more than arguing over the theory of sexuality. She's saving the world from collapse.

You'll have noticed during that fleeting glance cast in fear and excitement across the newsagent's top shelf that pornography loves the word *private*. The observation probably confirmed the link already deeply embedded in you between privacy and sex. It's no longer good form, as it seems to have been in Freud's time, to tell the small boy ostentatiously pulling and poking at himself in company that if he carries on like that it'll fall or be cut off. He's more likely to hear the gentle whisper, perhaps intensifying his fevered arousal, that what he's doing belongs *in private*. He might come to notice that only in the one privileged instance of naming the genital, or *privates*, is the adjective elevated to the status of noun.

A stream of direct and oblique messages from the adult world intimate a deep and enigmatic affinity between sex and privacy. The privacy of sex wasn't, you sensed, merely descriptive, couldn't be reduced to the banal fact of not being public. Newsagents put porn on the top shelf to keep it out of children's reach, and that distance separating your dangerous curiosity from its fulfilment measured the measureless space between the two worlds in which you had to live at once. A daylit world in which words and experiences were held in common, easily communicable, easily intelligible, cutting across the shared spaces of the classroom, the playground, the TV room. And a nocturnal world more real than any of this, more immediately felt in the intimate creases of the mind and body, yet also more inaccessible, incomprehensible. You'd have called it the adults' world in so far as it existed on the other side of the parental bedroom door, only you'd intuited that they were no more in secure possession of this unruly entity than you were, that in fact this was where their self-possession ended, where they no longer knew one another or themselves. The private spaces closed off to you in the outside world were only pale reflections of the regions in yourself you couldn't reach except by unwittingly drifting into them in waking or sleeping dreams.

Sex is private, then, not only in the well-worn sense that its proper place is on the other side of a closed door, but in the rarer sense of being essentially unshareable. Sex, for all it requires the real or fantasized presence of another, abandons you to yourself, to the untameable forces of pleasure and pain, to a region where common language, and its accompanying faith that your experience can be understood by someone else, run aground.

Perhaps, approaching adolescence, you found or were shown a porn mag by an older relative. You feigned disgust – no, not feigned, the disgust was as real as the voracious excitement – only to return to it when you knew it would be left unattended. You flicked feverishly through the fleshy orgy of pink and peroxide spread across the pages, through texts that seemed to congeal into viscous streams of meaningless obscenity under your watery gaze. A nauseous ecstasy unravelled your insides, scrambled the order of words and things.

You'd come to look at it again, and again, until your over-wrought frenzy gave way to a more clinical curiosity. The cata-strophic pile-up of scarlet fingernails, rolling blue eyeballs, prone apertures, angry protrusions, even the peremptory narra-tives precariously binding them together, start to come into discrete focus. Cheerleader orgies, fellating skiers, self-pleasuring shorthand typists – offices and cars and kitchens and triage rooms all hosting this infinitely variable combinatory of bodily entrances and exits, the innocent spaces of everyday life revealed as Chinese boxes concealing their own corrupted doubles.

At some point, it's hard to know exactly when, the excitement abruptly deflated. Perhaps at the moment you were caught in the aggressively direct gaze of one of the inflated women on display. Something about its seductive intent has a shaming effect. You are looking at me, her eyes say to you, and I know it. And soon enough that's what all the images are saying, whether they look at you or not. Under your gaze the delirious eye-rolling, the frenzied conjunctions of bodies are inexorably disenchanted by their preposterously wooden staginess. This is the harsh discovery of what you already knew, that these are exhibited bodies, knowing displays offered up to the gaze of anyone who wants to look, not just you. The breathless fantasy that you're peeking through a secret window carved for you alone into the walls of the most private is no longer sustainable. The illusion of a secret contract between your eye and these bodies shatters. Anyone can pick this up and look at it. Which somehow means it's not their privacy that's been violated, but yours. It's your desire, your dream life that's being raided here. Humiliating, finally – that all the while you think you're looking at it, pornography is looking at you.

Who told thee that thou wast naked? This is God's reproachful question to Adam, moments after his fateful ingestion of the wrong apple. It follows a previous question, equally vexed: *Where art thou?* An odd inquiry, surely, coming from an all-seeing and omniscient Creator. There's something at once poignant and understatedly hilarious in this moment of divine vulnerability, in God evoking the hapless dad scanning the park in horrified panic for the toddler who was 'just here, I swear', only a moment ago. *I was afraid because I was naked and I hid myself*, replies the newly mortified Adam, provoking that next question.

In asking Adam where he is, God registers his creation's new-found capacity to hide. Adam no longer belongs to a transparent

universe in which all is immediately visible. Something withdraws
from the universal reign of light, something that momentarily
eludes even God, Light itself. To recall Arendt, the world abruptly
divides itself at this moment into *things that should be shown and
things that should be hidden*. And the first things to be consigned
to the latter category have just been placed behind fig leaves,
inventing no less than privacy itself. *Where art thou?* Why are you
hiding? What are you hiding? To which the inevitable follow-up
question is, *Who told thee that thou wast naked?* Or: Who in hell
told you that you had something to hide?

The forbidden knowledge yielded by the serpent's apple, it
turns out, is firstly the existence of a concealed private self and
secondly the essential relation of that self to sex. Adam is returned
to God's vision, but irrevocably changed, a part of him forever
held back in darkness, obscured behind a fig leaf. Divine shock
registers a creation that is now irremediably divided – between
what should be shown and what hidden, between public and
private. The discovery of nakedness, and of human sexuality,
creates a pocket of obscurity in the world that not even God
can eliminate. From now on, God will have to disseminate and
enforce a complex network of regulations for the proper and
improper enjoyment of this newly discovered force called sex.
But in seeking thus to bring this force back under His sovereignty,
He's simultaneously acknowledging that it has already escaped,
that He doesn't possess it, that it can do things – adultery, incest,
the infinite array of perversions into which the sexual drive can
be directed – that defy His will.

So the opening chapters of Genesis, of the human race's most
enduring account of its own birth, tell you the human is born in
hiding, from God and himself alike. Adam is immortal, not yet
human as long as he can't see he has anything to hide, as long as
he believes that everything he'd want to see is already on display.

In placing their fig leaves, Adam and Eve mark themselves as obscure to themselves, as beings whose very nature is to conceal, disguise, dissimulate, giving birth to humanity itself in the process.

Perhaps this accounts for the profound appeal of the pre-lapsarian state to theologians, philosophers and poets down the ages, of a divine condition in which there's nothing to hide, and so nothing to suspect or fear, where what you see coincides entirely with what you get. This is how Milton conceives the blissful idyll of Adam and Eve's life in Eden. The Paradise of *wedded love* is a kind of total immersion in light: *Here Love his golden shaft employs, here lights/ His constant lamp.* Love is the means by which Adam attains divine unity and completeness, proof against his own insufficiency as a solitary being, *unity defective.* The light of paradisiacal Love banishes from the world any possibility of misunderstanding or frustration. It banishes, in short, desire, the want of something you don't have. In such a universe there can be no nakedness – that is, no state of lack, no difference between what you show and what you hide, between a true and a false self, and so no singular self. *Nor*, writes Milton, *those mysterious parts were then concealed/ Then was not guilty shame, dishonest shame/Of nature's works.*

The paradisiac language of man must have been one of perfect knowledge, writes Walter Benjamin in a beautiful and strange essay of 1916. Benjamin imagines an Edenic language which, like the bodies of Milton's Adam and Eve, conceals nothing. He compares this *blissful Adamite language-mind* with the reality of human language as we know it, the Babel of confused tongues, *empty prattle*, words, words, words. In the profane language of ordinary humans, words dissemble, deceive, manipulate and leave us in the dark. *Who told thee that thou wast naked?* Or: Who taught you that word *naked*? It is, as God's panic attests, a dangerous word, insinuating into language a suspicion from which it had been blissfully free, that what you say, like your fig-leaved body, hides as much as it shows. Words will now be to truth what clothes are to the body.

In the midst of all this sublimity, a cartoon frame pops into my mind: Snoopy, eyes raised heavenward in shame, sitting on a veterinary couch, his think bubble declaring, *It's embarrassing sitting here without any clothes on.* Someone once told me she loved *Peanuts* with the marked exception of Snoopy, whom she found creepy because he's neither human nor animal, but a sort of kink in the order of the world. I know what she means, though I suspect that's why he so captivates me. He parodies the sentimental myth of the animal as inhabiting an untroubled prelapsarian idyll – he sleeps and eats, as blithely indifferent to the human noise around him as one imagines the beasts tended by Adam. Until, that is, the human abruptly intrudes into the beagle and he's writing novels or going to court or hanging around campus looking for chicks. You imagine him as God complacently imagined Adam, as someone who doesn't know he doesn't have any clothes on, and then are as startled as God to discover he actually does know, and what's more is embarrassed by the fact. Snoopy does for animals what *Peanuts* as a whole does for kids – dispels the fantasy of an uncorrupted Eden some-where in the universe, a fantasy which all kids know, and many adults prefer not to know, is both idiotic and pernicious.

The kids of *Peanuts* inhabit, like the rest of us, a garden into which Satan is always surreptitiously wandering. For what Satan brings irrevocably into the garden, to plunge into Milton once again, is the fatally concealed motive, the withholding of the naked truth behind a duplicitous show of something else. Look at the language that follows him through *Paradise Lost* like a bad smell: darkness, shadow, obscurity, dimness. He slips into Eden *unespied*, a shape-shifter concealing himself among *the sportful herd / Of those four-footed kinds, himself now one, / Now other,* staking his human prey behind the eyes of lion or tiger. Into Eve's pure dreams he insinuates *distempered, discontented thoughts, / Vain hopes, vain aims, inordinate desires.* The serpent, his final and fateful guise, is *Fit vessel, fittest imp of fraud, in whom / To enter, and his dark suggestions hide / From sharpest sight.*

Before it brings cruelty and misery, Satan's entrance on to the scene of life brings privacy, a region of inner life into which light can't penetrate, hidden from sharpest, even from divine sight. Before he arrives, Adam and Eve know pleasure, but not desire, not, that is, the frustrating gap between a wish and its fulfilment. Milton imagines their erotic life as uninterrupted bliss, a bodily and spiritual union knowing no lack, no want of anything it doesn't already have. This vision of erotic fulfilment is Satan's *hell*, where he knows *neither joy nor love, but fierce desire, / . . . Still unfulfilled with pain of longing.* His final vengeance on his own pain is to get the envied couple to suffer it with him. *In lust they burn:* the moment the Satanic confusion of unfulfilled desire is felt by the newly fallen couple for the first time is surely the saddest in all of *Paradise Lost.* This, it tells you, is the destiny you're consigned to as a mortal and so sexual being, your *eyes how opened*, your *minds / How darkened.* You belong to a world in which everyone and everything, including you, is concealing their innermost reality.

Gaps – between what you show and hide, have and want, say and mean. Gaps are the strange non-spaces Satan insinuates into the texture of the world, catastrophically transforming it for eternity. Psychoanalysis is, in this respect, an essentially Satanic, or at least post-Satanic practice. It starts from the premise that you come into the world, like Satan, afflicted by *pain of longing*, dimly perceiving an internal need you're powerless to assuage, and that will stay with you for as long as you're alive. It describes a world within and without you replete with gaps – in love, in pleasure, in understanding – and seeks to relieve you, at least a little, of the Satanic rage these gaps provoke in you, to dispel the seductive and cruel fantasy that they could be eliminated, that somewhere an inner Paradise untainted by frustration and desire awaits if only you can find it.

Psychoanalysis works in the medium of language because it's through words that you discover *fierce desire* as your birthright. Words are the medium through which you both make sense of and become irremediably confused by your desires. *Words may be regarded as predestined to ambiguity*, as Freud writes in *The Interpretation of Dreams*. From his earliest to his latest writings, he insists that the failure of words to coincide with the things they name is a, if not the, central predicament of being human. You speak, as Lydia Davis shows in her story of the young woman who's really a fat old man, to externalize inner thoughts and feelings, only to discover that something, perhaps the very thing you most wanted to communicate, has been left behind in the passage from the silent matter of inner life to the noise of words. However hard you try to bring it to light, something always remains in the dark.

Nor those mysterious parts were then concealed / Then was not guilty shame, dishonest shame / Of nature's works.

We like to think we've come out of the dark ages of social and religious shame. But you have only to observe modern culture's relationship to the naked body to see how wildly optimistic a hope this is. Rationalists and libertarians have long enjoined us to throw off our bodily shame as the dead relic of a frightened and repressive past. And yet it survives, as indestructible and persistent as a horror movie monster.

You could imagine pornography and naturism as twin

solutions to the shame of the flesh – the invention of a shameless world by the former and of a world without shame by the latter. Shamelessness is the more paradoxical option, in so far as it's rooted in the simultaneous acknowledgement and defiance of shame. Porn starts from the premise that there are things you're not supposed to see, that we should be ashamed to show you and you should be ashamed to look at, but that we're both going to in spite or even because of all that. In this respect, it positions you as a concealed Satan, spying impotently on pleasures that aren't yours. Only unlike in Eden, the pornographic couple (or however many) know they're being spied on. This is what my adolescent self realized in a sudden and humiliating burst of shame: what I'm seeing can't be private, because if it was I couldn't logically be here looking at it. Porn catches you looking, catches you wanting to see what you shouldn't, and so brings back the very shame it claimed to override. It promises to let you in to the most private sanctum of experience, only to keep you out, to taunt you with the pleasure that isn't yours.

This is equally the effect of Steve McQueen's brilliantly un-comfortable, emphatically non-pornographic film *Shame*. I'm thinking in particular of the unthinking urgency with which the protagonist fires up his computer as soon as he sits or lies down, to navigate endless, punishingly repetitious vistas of sexual fantasy, intimated to us only via faint, histrionic moans. Such is your claustrophobic proximity to him in every frame, you find yourself less looking at than experiencing his predicament. Feeling the draining intensity of his despair, you stay with him in anticipation of the insight that might draw him out of the dark. But like the sister and lovers who try vainly to make contact with him, you find yourself instead being drawn further into the dark, mired in his irremediable desire for something he can't possess. The more he keeps you out, the more he exacerbates your painful itch to get closer, to see into his suffering. And the more you try to see, the blinder you feel.

But then this is his predicament exactly. However far he intrudes into the other's body and heart, he finds himself, like you watching him, on the wrong side of a screen. You start to suspect that he experiences the fleshly and the virtual other, the human in front of him and the figure on the screen, in essentially the same way – that is, as screens. There's no bodily contact so intimate, no skin so naked that it doesn't finally screen him out, leave him feeling he's missing the very thing that would make the difference.

Such, then, is the Satanic gaze of pornography, forever *unfulfilled with pain of longing*. The naturist vision, as its name implies, is more Edenic, or at least pseudo-Edenic. Milton reminds us that the vision of a sexual body untainted by shame is profoundly religious, a fantasy of a universe into which Satanic duplicity hasn't yet intruded. Naturism wants to restore you to that prelapsarian idyll of the body's *simplicity and spotless innocence*. It assures you that you have nothing to hide, that your body can be seen 'just as it is', without the distorting overlay of erotized perception that Adam's fig leaf intruded into Judeo-Christian culture and morality. There is a natural body distinct and separate from a sexual body.

Which seems plausible enough in theory. In theory, in the abstract, on paper, the distinction between a natural and a sexual body is perfectly intelligible and coherent. But try to sustain the distinction in thinking about concrete experience and it becomes more troublesome.

Take the example that so provoked D., of the baby at the breast, Freud's *prototype of every relation of love*. If you look at this bodily and emotional interchange between mother and baby as natural, it'll yield one kind of story: the baby feels hungry, so externalizes this feeling in a cry, which the mother responds to by offering him the breast. His hunger satisfied, the baby contentedly falls asleep.

But this bald sequence of events is barely a story at all, more a description of a nutritive instinct built into the natural order which could be seamlessly extended to many non-human animals. To stop the story here is to drain away its drama. There's no straightforwardly biological process in human experience – no experience, however 'natural', that doesn't secretly host the strange and unpredictable movement of unconscious life. For the French psychoanalyst Jean Laplanche, feeding a baby brings out the essentially double or *deceitful* nature of human life, deceitful because it's always smuggling unknown currents of sensation and emotion into the most apparently innocent of transactions: *simultaneous with the feeding function's achievement of satisfaction in nourishment, a sexual process begins to appear. Parallel with feeding there is a stimulation of lips and tongue by the nipple and the flow of warm milk.*

Whenever you watch a baby feed at the breast, you're bearing witness to more than the satisfaction of his appetite. You're also seeing his initiation into psychic and bodily pleasure and frustration. As he grows, an initially incomprehensible chaos of sensations comes increasingly into focus. Variations both subtle and dramatic in texture and temperature, in sound and vision, and in his own bodily responses, insinuate themselves into his experience of feeding. And all of these factors are further shaped by the inner states of the mother. The hedonism of the gourmet and the self-destruction of the anorexic alike alert us to the fact that feeding was and is never just feeding. Food is the bearer of messages that are always more than nutritive, that express ever-changing configurations of the feeder's love, hate, generosity, resentment, patience, frustration, attentiveness, distraction, joy and misery.

To complicate the story still further, the drama of mother and baby always involves more than two players. Their mutual absorption is prone to all kinds of interruption; father enters the room, or the mother's mind. What difference will he make? Will his love for their baby leave her feeling more deeply secure in his affections or suddenly displaced from them? Will his indifference enforce or inhibit her dreamy immersion in the world of her baby? And of course the scene is liable to become more populated still, with real and fantasized siblings and grandparents and friends intruding into the imperceptible space between breast and mouth, supporting, competing, demanding – ensuring he takes in more than just milk.

Perhaps there's a clue here as to why the tired controversy over breastfeeding in public is forever rearing its ugly head. You may rightly deplore the constipated prurience of those who object. And yet there's something about the defence of breastfeeding as the most natural act in the world that, not unlike the naturist's defence of the naturalness of the naked body, misses the point. Intuited in the inarticulate anxieties of the objectors is a sense that nothing in the human world is merely natural. Nature can never appear in isolation from the many, usually confused meanings invested in it.

The proponents of naturism or the right to breastfeed in public tend to appeal to the distinction between the sexual and the non-sexual body, which is then overlain by another, more or less explicitly moralized distinction between those who do and don't grasp the distinction. Everyone, goes the argument, barring the inevitable minority of creeps and weirdos (about whom nothing can be done), knows the difference between a breast intended to arouse and one intended to feed, or between ordinary and sexualized nakedness. 'I kiss my kids. I do not *perv* on my kids.' Context, in other words, is everything: where the breast is, what it's doing, how it's displayed will tell all but the most diseased eye how to see it.

This argument can't fail to trouble a psychoanalyst, or indeed anyone primed to suspect appearances. Context is where and how a thing appears, the public setting in which it's perceived. It is, undoubtedly, very important – but to say it's everything is almost literally to flatten out the world, to reduce it to its observable surface. Freud introduced the idea of the uncanny to give body to the inchoate feeling that occasionally comes over you when a familiar object or person appears inexplicably strange. There's always something hidden, he suggests, and never more so than when you're sure there isn't. To insist on the naturalness of the naked body is to screen out the strangeness of what we think we know.

Walking along a Cornish beach some years ago, absently dodging the wetsuited surfers and toddlers and sandcastles caught in the long shadow cast by the inhumanly vast sandstone cliffs, I looked up to find myself at the edge of a naturist section I hadn't known (you'll be justified in raising an eyebrow at this 'not knowing') was there. As the scene came into focus, a tall grey-headed man filled my field of vision, his professorial silver wire-frame glasses alone betraying his citizenship of the post-Edenic world. Perhaps it was my admiration of his easy pleasure in his own flesh shading into Satanic envy, but the more unselfconscious he seemed, the more self-conscious I privately accused him of being, as though he were the star of some preposterous anthropological exhibit called Man in His Natural Habitat.

And then he cheerfully strode over to what I took to be his wife and adolescent children, whom I remember, quite possibly faultily, as all wearing swimming costumes. But I'm in no doubt about the turquoise bikini his daughter was wearing as he took her by the hand to stroll at the edge of the surf, or the nervy shyness of her smile as she stared distractedly into the waves. Fed into the busy click and whirr of my imagination, she was no more than sixteen. She was wearing the bikini to contain the new and unsettling spill of her flesh over its frame, to contain the sadness and excitement and confusion of its vanishing childishess. She was embarrassed of and angry with her father for denying there's anything to hide when it was so painfully self-evident for her that there is. If she had a natural body distinct from a sexual one, she knew nothing about it, not for herself and certainly not for her father. In fact, the idea felt to her like a faintly cruel joke, a bit like the pendulous cylinder of tissue she was being encouraged to both see and not notice, as though she was being denied the right to be excited and disturbed. Hands touching, eyes averted – Adam strolling through Eden, failing to notice Eve has been banished and is now his daughter.

Of course, all this may be nothing more than the wild and presumptive musing of an off-duty shrink. But the scene gave it to me to imagine, and you certainly don't need to be a shrink to intuit how much bodies and families hide, from themselves and others, not least when they're on display.

D.'s objection to Freud is that he *sexualizes* – maternity, childhood, affection – experiences which should be free of any taint of the sexual. Here as in so much else, Freud seems to be the avant-garde of one of the most reviled tendencies of modern culture. As he wasn't shy to point out, almost no one before him was willing or able to talk about the sexuality of children. *So far as I know*, he would write at the beginning of the second of his *Three Essays*, 'Infantile Sexuality', *not a single author has clearly recognised the existence of a sexual drive in childhood*. From this rather startling omission, Freud will begin his audacious and notorious project to establish *the existence of a sexual drive in childhood* as the trauma that conditions every phase of human life.

His compelling and infuriating evidence will continue to be that no one wants to talk about it, think about it or even acknowledge it, as though its pervasive and near-total concealment were the most luminous attestation to its existence. Freud goes further still. It's not that you know about infantile sexuality and prefer to pretend otherwise for reasons of good taste and decorousness. On the contrary, you really don't know about it, because like any psychic trauma its most remarkable feature is its vulnerability to *amnesia*. Infantile sexuality is a sort of footprint in the sand, its tracks erased as soon as they're laid down. *Infantile amnesia*, writes Freud, *which turns everyone's childhood into something like a prehistoric epoch and conceals from him the beginnings of his own sexual life, is responsible for the fact that in general no importance is attached to childhood in the development of sexual life.*

Given the swelling, media-fuelled tidal wave of panic and indignation directed against consumerism's sexualizing of children, to be amnesiac in this regard seems these days both impermissible culturally and impossible practically. Impressionable boys scanning the magazine racks for the latest wholesome dispatches from Nintendo and the Premier League are assailed by the conspiratorially winking eyes and cleavage of the air-brushed harem marketed to their adolescent elders. The distance now separating their geography homework from the virtual garden of earthly delights is as infinitesimal as a click. Boys are perpetually in danger of stumbling unawares into a dangerously unknown adult world. But girls, it would seem, are being actively and ruthlessly seduced into it. The fashion, diet, entertainment and even the aesthetic surgery industries are all adapting the desires and anxieties they generate to the fragile scale of their unripe bodies and minds.

I had a peculiar confrontation with this reality towards the end of the last century on a sultry day in north London. Dragging my feet along the edge of a teeming park, basking in the drowsy mid-afternoon heat, I noticed a car unloading on the block ahead. A sprightly little figure leapt out as an adult body bent into it. A band of pink cotton round her waist sprang upward in exact synchronicity with the rest of her. She landed, squatted, straightened, swayed her hips left and right and spun, so that by the time I was close enough to make her out she was facing me, her impossibly straightened arm pointing right at me in seductive concert with her one open eye. She held the pose, and my stupefied self, in the same freeze frame for an eternal half-second before leaping abruptly back up and, left hand behind head, lavender-tipped right hand curled on her tiny ribcage, thrust her pelvis back and forth in a climactic flourish, eyes still locked on mine. They continued to follow me as I drew a nervily wide semicircle round her. It had been a long time since I'd tried to run away from a seven-year-old.

Meanwhile, in the last few seconds of my personal audience with this miniature Britney avatar, an adult head had emerged from beneath the car's roof to reveal a wearily exasperated mother's face, barely mustering the will and energy to shout, 'Amanda, I have told you to stop this,' at the little girl, who merely smiled and batted her eyelids in response. 'Sorry,' her mother said to me, in a tone and look both irritable and defeated. I grinned, nodded, stuttered moronically the words, 'No no no, she's, erm, really . . .' and broke off, which made no difference as by now they'd both lost interest.

I was unsettled, seriously creeped out. Only now, at a distance of thirteen or fourteen years from this fleeting encounter, do I ask myself, by what? By the undeniable reality and raw immediacy of what Freud calls infantile sexuality? Actually, no.

What I'd seen had very little to do with the polymorphous inner chaos of excited curiosity, arousal and aggression to which Freud gives that name. The creepiness of this little dance routine, of the entire spectacle of marketed pre-teen female sexuality, of the *Playboy* crop-tops, the be-thonged Barbies, the padded bras, the pole-dancing lessons, the beauty pageants, lies rather in its artifice.

The Day-Glo aesthetic of sexualized childhood holds a grotesque mirror up, not to infantile sexuality, but to adult sexuality and its impoverishment. It shows us in miniature the bodily and psychic emptiness of contemporary consumer sexuality, a sexuality cut off from its infantile sources – dead, inorganic, curiously *a*sexual.

There's a clue to this state of affairs in the word itself: to sexu-al*ize* is to render sexual what previously wasn't. Condensed in that word is a sentimental fantasy of childhood as an idyll of prelapsarian innocence helplessly vulnerable to Satanic corruption. A malignant external force called sexuality is threatening to spoil the spotless purity of the child's original state.

When this issue is framed as a struggle between the crusading protectors and the nefarious exploiters of childhood, what's missed is the secret complicity between the two. If sexuality has no infantile form, but enters only belatedly on to the scene of life at adolescence in a flurry of camply choreographed poses from a lads' mag cover, then the outraged protesters and cynical marketers are in unwitting agreement. Both can conceive of sexuality only as an external phenomenon, a kind of prosthetic that can be put on and off at will like a push-up bra.

The substance of sex, on this model, is not what it hides but what it shows, not what it withholds but what it puts on display. In spite of the facile conviction that we've heard it all before, we continue to turn a deaf ear to what Freud still has to tell us. Our infallibly knowing, sexually liberated culture remains as amnesiac as ever about infantile sexuality – which should be understood as the sexuality not so much of the child as of the child you continue to be. Infantile sexuality is the restless presence in you of untameable, alien desires and impulses, of forces you rightly fear because they threaten your bodily and psychic undoing. You like your sexuality where you can see it. If you can't, you prefer to say it's not there.

5

Cancelling Yourself Out

Yom Kippur, or in the joyless English translation, bereft of the original's eerily transportive power, the Day of Atonement. I'm fifteen, standing over the kitchen bin, scraping away the bones of a boiled chicken, tongue rolling itself absently over the slick film spread across the roof of my mouth by its blandly succulent flesh. It's late afternoon, and these oily residues will be the last intake of food before tomorrow evening. The knot of my tie, fastened with the same inexplicably manic anxiety that always infuses the hour preceding this, *the holiest day of the year* (a phrase I'll only ever be able to hear in the reproachful hush of parents and Hebrew teachers), strains against my Adam's apple.

Soon enough I'm in synagogue, following the wryly contemptuous gaze of the regulars on the twice-a-year types, all couture and earnestness. The irony of Yom Kippur is that it enjoins you to transcend the body, yet rarely do you feel yourself more riveted to its merciless demands, wishes and frustrations. The roughly eleven glasses of water ritually downed in the misguided hope of being shored up against thirst now stretch the lining of my bloated stomach and press on my angry bladder.

As evening gives way to day, so this lumbering over-satiation yields to hunger and fatigue. The overawed language of sin and redemption, with its humbling intimations of your infinitesimal place in God's cosmic order, is blasphemously overlain by flashes of gluttony – hallucinatory draughts of iced ginger beer, milky coffee, fried fish, lemon cake. I was meant to rise above the body in the name of spirit, but the flesh pulls me vindictively back down. The seat's flat mahogany back and hard leather buttons chafe and poke the bones and buttocks craving rest, turning my body into a dissonant symphony of its parts' competing resentments.

This year I'm sitting alone, events having scattered my companions of past years to Zion, or Manchester. Gazing listlessly through the stained glass to the profane autumnal grey beyond, I listen to this sullen internal grumbling with graceless tolerance. The afternoon service is starting, meaning the end, and restoration to my eating self, is in sight. What's more, the room is nicely airy, most worshippers having cleared out till the concluding service, leaving behind a few stray, largely elderly men sitting upright, staring into their lowered eyelids.

At this point a congregant ascends to the dais to recite the Book of Jonah. I turn to the announced page, seeing only a string of dead letters where the title sits. But I'm sprung from my inertia by the surprising realization that I've never read this agreeably diminutive Book. No doubt I was told its story a hundred times, but I retain only a picture-book illustration held aloft by the teller, of a little man, barefoot and bearded, seated at a stiff right angle in the centre of a blue oblong. Years later I'll discover that Orwell's famous essay imagines Jonah ensconced in *yards of blubber*, cosily insulated from the turbulent noise of the world outside. But to my child's eye, the image in the picture-book was anything but cosy. I see him suspended above the floor of the whale's stomach, an image, for all its constrictive enclosure, of consignment to a vertiginous nothingness, to a darkness which, once experienced, holds you forever, regardless of whether or not you emerge from it.

All of a sudden I'm reading with an urgency that briefly banishes even hunger. God, I read, tells Jonah to proclaim against the wickedness of the *great city of Nineveh. But Jonah rose up to flee unto Tarshish from the presence of the LORD; and he went down to Joppa, and found a ship going to Tarshish; so he paid the fare thereof and went down into it, to go with them unto Tarshsish, from the presence of the LORD.*

I'm startled by what I can't yet name as a confrontation with an image, an inverse reflection of the compliant self with whom I've come to be confused, by myself as much as others. I'm here, in so far as I've thought about the question at all, because God says I should be, reading the story of a man for whom what God says is an invitation to do the opposite. God says, Go east and proclaim, in response to which Jonah goes west and proclaims nothing. It's hard to imagine a purer expression of adolescent bravura, a door more loudly slammed on the paternal Voice. I'm speechless with admiration, vicarious triumph and a little shame.

The heroic futility of Jonah's gesture thrills me. His daring to seek a place beyond the reach of God's oppressive gaze seems to me a supreme imaginative act, deepened by the fact that there is no such place and he knows it. As though to remind Jonah there's no escaping Him, God stirs the sea to a *mighty tempest*, inducing terror in the ship's crew. But, having descended *into the innermost parts of the ship*, where he lies *fast asleep*, Jonah remains untouched by God's storming rage.

You probably know how the story goes from here. Jonah will be woken, will persuade the ship's reluctant crew to *cast me forth into the sea*, will be swallowed and reside in the belly of *a great fish* for three days and nights, will offer up thanksgiving for his salvation, will be *vomited out . . . upon the dry land*, will comply with God's second call to proclaim His word to Nineveh, will become angry when the Ninevites' repentance moves God to mercy, will remonstrate with Him for sparing those for whom Jonah had prophesied death, will become angry once again when granted and then deprived of the protective shade of a gourd grown and withered by God.

For my parched and hungry adolescent self, the flurry of incident after Jonah is cast overboard is little more than a diverting postscript. My head may have been swept along with the furious tide of events, but my heart has stayed behind with the man who refused this descent into blind, frenzied action, who preferred to go to sleep.

That, I marvel to myself, is surely what rebellion means. Everywhere torrents of rage, righteous or nihilistic, threaten to burst the bubble of privileged conformism from which I peer out in fearful fascination. The green Mohicans and studded leathers of street punks, the numbingly shrill rhetoric of student militancy, the waves of bloody protest in inner cities and mining villages, all these voices and bodies staked in making the world feel the reality of their anger. And I do feel it, with horror, incomprehension, a little awe. I feel it with the impersonal shudder induced by a tornado or earthquake viewed from afar, with the terror you feel in the face of some destructive force that has nothing to do with you.

But Jonah's silence has everything to do with me. The impulse, in the face of the persecuting menace of being perpetually seen and judged, to annul all contact, to disappear from all others and even from myself – that's the kind of defiance that sings in my gut, that I feel as unmistakably mine. *What meanest thou that thou sleepest?* the shipmaster demands of Jonah incredulously. In his blind panic, the shipmaster alights very perceptively on exactly what's most infuriating about sleep – that it doesn't mean anything. In the face of a storm so fearfully meaningful, his question seems to imply, how is it that Jonah can do something so provokingly meaningless?

Not all sleep is meaningless. The Bible is full of meaningful sleepers, or dreamers, their minds febrile chambers of private communication with God. But Jonah doesn't dream. Down in the bowels of the ship, he puts himself beyond the reach of God's word, oblivious to the destruction He's wreaking above decks. Jonah's sleeping mind receives no messages.

Dreams, writes Freud in 1917, *only show us the dreamer in so far as he is **not** sleeping*. If the sleeper had her way, he suggests, she'd withdraw all interests and investments from the world, would retreat to a point zero of psychic activity. God can talk to a dreamer, but not to a sleeper. The dream is a kind of aperture in sleep, letting a bit of the outside in, maintaining some degree of activity in the mind. When the aperture closes, so does all commerce with the world and with oneself. The twelve-word prayer Jews are enjoined to recite on waking declares thanks to God for having *restored mercifully my soul within me*. Sleep, in other words, is a temporary flight of the soul (Greek *psyche*), a bit of death.

What meanest thou that thou sleepest? The question will be familiar to every adolescent who's felt its bellowed outrage rumble through their half-slumbering body and tried to muffle its echo with the tug of a duvet. In adolescence, wakefulness can feel like the onslaught of a vindictive enemy or raging storm, to be kept out at all costs. Seen in this light, don't an adolescent's abrupt shifts between wild agitation and sullen inertia appear peculiarly rational?

Like Jonah, the adolescent is perpetually fending off furious demands from all directions, inducing a profound disturbance in his internal equilibrium. He finds himself split between the impulse to embrace the state of excited agitation and the equally urgent need to annul it, to take refuge in the ship's hold of empty, dreamless sleep. Adolescence concentrates the essential dilemma of the living being as Freud came to see it: to expand outward into the noisy excitement of more life or contract inward into the peaceful quiescence of less.

From the very beginning, Freud contended that the primary task of the psyche was to minimize its own excitement. The imperative of self-preservation encoded in the human species endows the self with an aversion to anything that disturbs its internal equilibrium. Even the sexual drive, with its impulsion towards bodily pleasure, is ultimately a way of getting rid of psychic and physical tension. But in his startling essay of 1920, *Beyond the Pleasure Principle*, Freud took a leap beyond his idea. Written in the shadow of the unprecedented mass slaughter of the First World War, during which he'd seen his own sons called to the Front, the book offers a haunting vision of death as a perpetual presence, insidious and imperceptible, in life.

Five chapters in, Freud tells an extraordinary, extravagantly speculative story of the origins of life. The prehistoric world he conjures up evokes the formless void of the Genesis creation narrative, a landscape of dead matter suddenly nudged into animation *by the action of a force of whose nature we can have no conception*. But where the biblical story sees life beget more life, Freud's version imagines matter experiencing the intrusion of life as an unwelcome disturbance of its peace. As soon as it is stirred into life, matter wants to *return to an inanimate state*, to restore its unbroken sleep. Where in the sacred version life once born wants to *go forth and multiply*, in Freud's blasphemous revision it wants to go backward and *cancel itself out*. The first drive, he suggests, isn't erotic, expansive, venturesome, but self-depleting, silent, deathly.

I'm reminded of Jonah's anguished (not to say adolescent) refrain when the sleep he yearns for is interrupted by the demand to act: *Better is my death than my life*. Traditionally prophets are what we might call life-driven. They submit ecstatically to the command to extend God's dominion, founding and growing great nations and sacred institutions. They partake in what Freud calls the life drive's impulsion to *ever larger unities*. Isn't Jonah's prophetic journey a kind of darkly comic inversion of the wildly expansive missions of Abraham, Jesus, Mohammed? He's the rare prophet who prefers to found nothing, say nothing, do nothing. His protest is poignantly simple and lovably human: please, can't you just let me sleep?

Yet Jonah's inner state is a good deal more complicated than mere laziness. The paradox of his first response to God is its single-minded passion. He heads in the opposite direction he's commanded, and descends into the silent anonymity of sleep, without any apparent hesitation or deliberation. I'm tempted to say he's driven to sleep. Perhaps that sounds like a glaring contradiction. One is driven to succeed or to protest or to kill or even to madness or despair, but not to sleep. Unless, that is, Freud's strange and disturbing thought that the very first drive begins in the urge *to cancel itself out* is right.

A story by Henry James comes to mind. More than once, alluding to 'The Beast in the Jungle' has moved my interlocutor to tell me how much they like or dislike Kipling. It may be that James mischievously courted this confusion. He was a great admirer of Kipling, and the story was published only a few years after the second *Jungle Book*. The title's echo invites associations with colonial adventurism, the heroic romance of imperial Britain. Kipling exemplifies storytelling as a life-driven enterprise in precisely Freud's sense. Like the project of Empire itself, Kipling's literary world draws together disparate elements from the human, animal and physical world and binds them into *ever larger unities*. Like the Empire itself, his stories aggrandize action, growth, development.

Seen in this light, James's title reads like a piece of radical irony. It isn't about great white hunters or daring leaps into dangerous places. Its jungle is an oppressively grey London, its Beast a pale illusion in the mind of its protagonist. The story tells of a man who, following a premonition from his *earliest time* of a catastrophe lying in wait – the Beast of the title – suspends all actions or decisions of any significance. He suspends, in other words, life itself, and this will turn out to be the very catastrophe he's spent his entire life trying to fend off.

But this summary version threatens to turn James's story into some folksy homily. Don't worry, it might never happen. Life's for living, so make the most of it. Lovers and haters of James alike will know that he doesn't do homilies. The great paradox that takes 'The Beast in the Jungle' beyond the realm of the cautionary tale is its presentation of John Marcher's lifelong refusal of life's passions as itself a singularly mad passion.

It is, after all, a love story of a kind. As bewitched as Marcher himself by his secret conviction, May Bartram becomes his sole confidante and companion in the eerily static journey of watching and waiting for the catastrophe to come: *'I'll watch with you,'* she solemnly avows. The couple forge a bond at least as deep and intense as any marriage, yet depleted of marriage's erotic foundation. It's a bond devoted not to enriching and growing itself into an ever larger unity, but to depriving and diminishing itself.

One of the most striking of the many intricate webs of imagery James weaves through the story is a motif of the absence of colour. Marcher carries his inner state of *perpetual suspense* with such quiet discretion, he appears to himself and others a model of disinterested civility and good sense. *This was why*, writes James, *he had such good – though possibly such rather colourless – manners.*

In the course of the story May becomes fatally ill. Marcher visits her in her cold drawing room one early spring morning to find her skin *almost as white as wax*. It's as though their courtship, forged in the holding back of life and love, has to end in death rather than union. Colour is the element in things that both literally and figuratively brings them to life. Marcher and May's bond is undoubtedly passionate, but a *blanched* passion, drained of the colour that would nourish it. It's a passion for *nothing*, another word James uses with the near-obsessive insistence of the Shakespeare of *King Lear*.

Marcher beseeches May to tell him what she knows that he doesn't. *'You know something that I don't,'* he tells her. *'You've shown me that before.'* *'I've shown you, my dear, nothing,'* she replies. Later, as she nears death, she asks him if he hasn't yet worked out his secret – *'Don't you know – now?'*, to which Marcher can only reply, *'Now? . . . I know nothing.'* Marcher and May are united in the bond of nothingness, in a passion for the depletion of passion. When May pledges herself to watch, she gives herself over to a kind of internal sleep, to a draining of colour from the face of life, a loss of all creative and erotic investments, to be sustained till death does them part.

So perhaps the title's reference to a beast isn't so ironic after all. There is a drive at work in Marcher and May which possesses them with all the animal desire you'd give to love or revenge or success, a drive seeking dreamless sleep rather than dream-fuelled life. The French psychoanalyst Piera Aulagnier, like Freud, sees this drive to nothingness as older and more fundamental than the drive to live and create. In order to live, she points out, you have to want things you don't yet have. For the infant in its earliest, unformed state, this desire is felt as an unbearable tension. The most infantile and primitive layer of your psyche, says Aulagnier, can't tolerate any reminder that it isn't self-sufficient, that it *might find itself in a state of lack.* There is in this sense an essential resistance to living in you, in so far as to live is to lack. Your deepest wish is to eliminate this sense of lack. This wish, writes Aulagnier, *is the major scandal of psychic functioning: . . . the original presence of a rejection of living in favour of the search for a state of quiescence, of* **non-desire**, *which remains the aim, unknown, but always at work, of desire.* What you secretly want more than anything else is not to want at all.

But do we really desire the noiseless sleep of Jonah's ship's hold, the colourless caution of Marcher's half-life? To withdraw into an impermeable carapace of nothingness – this is privacy taken too far, no more a model for living than the permanent, garish visibility of a Katie Price.

There's an impulse in you to quell all desires, needs and frustrations, to put an end to everything that disturbs your internal peace and equilibrium. You feel it when you respond to the alarm's rude awakening by burying your head in the pillow and denying, at least for a moment, the claim of the day. But that impulse isn't, ordinarily, the whole story. Freud's death drive is closely succeeded by, and must always coexist with, an erotic drive, a drive to live, grow and change. If you're not in the grip of a morbid depression, you'll soon enough lift your groggy head and look for what the day can offer to make up for your lost peace.

In *The Human Condition*, the very book in which she argues for the necessity of a properly private space, Hannah Arendt alerts us to the semantic links between privacy and *privation.* For the ancients, the word *meant literally a state of being deprived of something, and even of the highest and most human of man's capacities.*

And perhaps the most obvious 'something' we'd be deprived of by a retreat into absolute privacy is contact with others.

Jonah and Marcher each retreat from the world because the day outside offers only nameless terrors. What they have in common is the sense of being subject to a traumatically agitating call, a mortal threat waiting to pounce, *'possibly destroying'*, says Marcher, *'all further consciousness, possibly annihilating me'*. Only when the common world outside has the character of a malevolent intrusion does the drive to uninterrupted privacy start to take over. Only then might you want to pre-empt the Beast by annihilating your own psychic life, taking flight into the unrelieved blankness of sleep or colourless life.

The privacy Jonah and Marcher aspire to is a traumatized privacy, a bid to fence off the self from the other's intrusions, to immunize the mind and body from feeling too much. Marcher's tragedy is less that he can't love than that he's severed from any felt experience of love. When he breaks down before May's grave at the end of the story, he discovers that his passion for her has been lurking in him all the while, only cut off from all consciousness. The dangers of need and desire frighten him to the point that he makes himself impervious to their pains and pleasures alike.

In September 2009, the legal firm Carter Ruck raised what would come to be known as a super-injunction to prohibit reporting of its client Trafigura's internal inquiry into the 2006 Côte d'Ivoire toxic waste dump scandal. Some 30,000 Ivoireans had sought urgent medical attention after half a million litres of unprocessed waste containing lethal levels of hydrogen sulphide were dumped in the port of Abidjan.

The super-injunction was increasingly used by celebrities seeking to prevent similarly unwelcome revelations. The ordinary legal injunction was a means of preventing publication of particular facts or allegations about its claimant. The super-injunction adds a further layer of interdiction on this first one: not only can you not know what people are saying about me, you can't know the fact of their saying it. The super-injunction goes beyond the insistence that my secrets are mine alone, to deprive them of their very existence. It turns me into Mellifont, the James character who when unseen by others simply ceases to be at all. The super-injunction renders me the sum of what you can see, abolishing speculation that I might be any more or less. It conjures the fantasy of a gapless, fully integral being unencumbered by the dissonance that comes with the possession of an inner life.

You know from the oozing sacks of landfill you push into your wheelie bins that modern consumer capitalism is haunted by a nether side you'd prefer not to see. This is what Trafigura sought to conjure out of existence. But when the super-injunction is sought for a celebrity rather than a corporation, doesn't private life take over the role of unspeakable toxic waste? Dirt, shit – the tabloid synonyms for scandalous secrets converge exactly with the logic of Carter Ruck, designating private life as malodorous waste to be neutralized and disowned like so much raw sewage.

Concealed inside the furious conflict between the tabloid's will to expose and the super-injunction's drive to annul the dirt is a tacit agreement that our private lives are a source of shame and disgust. Both versions tacitly accede to the reduction of private life to the dirty secrets hidden behind the door, revealing who and what you really are. Transposed to the realm of celebrity culture, the super-injunction effectively invites you to imagine yourself as Trafigura, a corporate brand with a clean public face behind which hide the most sinister and venal forces. The war over privacy comes to be defined by the question of ownership, of who has rightful title over the dirt no one and everyone wants.

So when, in the noisiest episode in the super-injunction saga, Ryan Giggs took out a self-defeating super-injunction to prevent the reporting of his various adulteries, he aroused precisely the fantasy he wanted to suppress, that behind the bar on reporting lay the rapacious sexual glutton he really is. Giggs sought, like Mellifont (though evidently less successfully), to disappear seamlessly into his wholesome public persona. The super-injunction was his bid for ownership rights over his private life, in the name of protecting his public fame and, inevitably, the revenue it generates. Instead it became an exemplary attestation to the vanity of trying to dictate what others see when they look at you. Perhaps if Giggs had merely kept his own silence rather than seeking to impose it on everyone else, he might have seen that his private life couldn't be exhausted by his dirty secrets. And perhaps those impulses of sexual gluttony, opportunism and emotional destructiveness he sought to disown might have been less readily projected on to his lover, Imogen Thomas. Projections of this kind, suggests Melanie Klein, are the means by which you dump the most abject and unwanted parts of yourself in someone else. Left stranded alone in the blinding light of the paparazzi's flashgun, Thomas became a kind of Abidjan for the inner toxicity of Giggs, the tabloids and the rest of us.

Tabloid intrusion and the super-injunction alike treat private life as a prize to be captured or a possession to be withheld. Both options screen out the possibility that your private life may be what no one, not even you, can possess, that it's the elusive element in you which, diffused through your very being, is everywhere and nowhere, neither here nor there. Perhaps this is what provokes both the tabloid rage to expose it and the super-injunction's zeal to black it out. Both induce the singular self to disappear, to take cover inside a public face and descend into a sleep so deep not even God can reach it.

Jonah's sleep and the celebrity's super-injunctions are both forms of inert protest, passive rebellions against the demands and encroachments of others. When the singularity of your bodily and emotional experience, the place of what British analyst D. W. Winnicott calls with deceptive plainness the True Self, is felt as dangerous, the self will do all it can to cut itself off from it, to take refuge in the relative impersonality of the external world and its demands. This is what it means to be overtaken by your False Self – to live in a state of lifeless compliance.

It's easy enough to imagine the psychoanalyst's consulting room becoming a sealed-off asylum, insulated from the incursions of the external world and everyone in it. Easy enough to imagine the couch functioning like the bed in Jonah's ship's hold, affording the patient the literal or figurative respite of dreamless sleep. Or to imagine the analyst taking on the role of May Bartram, enlisted with quiet sadism to watch his patient slowly but inexorably drain her life away. Some people come to analysis unconsciously primed to do with you exactly what they've done with everyone else to whom they matter: cut you off even and especially as they're speaking and listening to you.

For the very reason I'm tempted to delete that last sentence, I'll let it stand. It betrays my frustrated susceptibility to blame the patient for their wariness and suspicion of me, my motives and interests. Perhaps I'm not the only analyst to get snagged occasionally in the fantasy of my own benevolence, to lament a patient's unwillingness to perceive and trust it, as though all would be well if only she did. If I'm not unduly self-punishing about it, I can feel oddly touched by the persistence in me of a child's ingenuous vanity, this irrational conviction in the essential goodness of what I am and do.

But perhaps we psychoanalysts are prone to feel too much at home in this fantasy of our benignity. This isn't to say we're not alive to the many ways in which a treatment can come undone. But these pitfalls are invariably ascribed to one of two elements: the analyst or the patient. The story is always a variant on one of two scenarios: I the analyst tried to give the patient something good but she proved too envious or sadistic or masochistic or self-punishing or perverse or phobic or paranoid to receive it. Or the patient tried to communicate something essential which some spot of deafness in my mind's ear – diagnostic or emotional or erotic or aggressive – rendered inaudible.

Psychoanalysts will almost always prefer to think a treatment's failed because it's been let down in some way by one of its participants than to imagine psychoanalysis itself is at fault. I can doubt my capacity to give or the patient's to take, but to doubt the worthiness of the gift itself comes perilously close to blasphemy. Many psychoanalysts since Freud have been interested in why people are inclined to hate psychoanalysis – to reject its ideas, to resist its clinical methods. But I'm not sure any of them before or since Winnicott has really taken seriously the possibility that they have a point.

In doing psychoanalysis . . . I aim at being myself and behaving myself. In my first encounters with Winnicott's writing, I found myself infuriated with this disarming simplicity of tone, so direct as to render itself weirdly gnomic. But I've come to love his style's wily interlacing of unapologetic authority and unaffected humility. A sentence like that one (which opens his 1962 essay 'The Aims of Psycho-Analytical Treatment') can be written only by someone with as passionate a faith in his limitations as in his capacities. To be and behave oneself is an oddly paradoxical aim for an analyst, somehow coinciding intense modesty and grand ambition, conceiving the task as entirely ordinary and yet impossibly difficult to define, let alone perform.

Winnicott's faith in psychoanalysis is strong enough not to preclude real suspicion of its intentions and effects. He hears a certain truth in the wordless protest of my fellow party guest that too many analysts are prone to ignore or dismiss. *We can understand the hatred people have of psychoanalysis*, he writes in his great 1963 essay 'Communicating and Not Communicating Leading to a Study of Certain Opposites', *which has penetrated a long way into the human personality, and which provides a threat to the human individual in his need to be secretly isolated*.

The analyst, invested by his patient with the power to reach into her ownmost self, is liable to be experienced as God to her Jonah – tracking her into her most guarded and vulnerable corners, smoking her unconscious out of its hole. I'm reminded of a patient's words to me: 'You remember so much I want to forget. I should find that reassuring. But I don't.' Perhaps we analysts are yet to learn the lesson Emmy von N. taught Freud: the unconscious wants to *tell what it has to say* – that is, to set the terms on which it will reveal itself, to emerge in its own time and space. It wants to speak in its own voice, not answer someone else's questions.

I get the sense that Jonah would be much more open to God if He didn't harass him like an intrusively persecuting parent, if He weren't forever at him to go there and do this, weren't perpetually teaching him one triumphal lesson or another about His sovereign power. This, in any case, is Winnicott's point about the patient: don't dazzle her with the brilliance (or in his own word, dripping with very English suspicion, the 'cleverness') of your insight, don't display your power to drag her unconscious into the light when what she might most need is for you to provide a little protective darkness, a space in which she and her unconscious can work things out for themselves.

Winnicott is, in a way, simply picking up on a basic feature of Freud's dreaming, joking, slipping unconscious: it wants both to hide and to be found. Dreams are the chosen language of the unconscious because they simultaneously send and encode messages to your waking self. They present you with your most urgent and powerful private wishes in a foreign language. Like proper adolescents, they want you to hear exactly what they have to say and to fuck off and leave them alone.

So it's no coincidence that the adolescent, along with the artist, embodies for Winnicott the irresolvable paradox of the private self. *In the artist of all kinds*, he writes, *I think one can detect an inherent dilemma, which belongs to the co-existence of two trends, the urgent need to communicate and the still more urgent need not to be found.* You cannot be reduced to the sum of your visible behaviours. Alongside the self you show the world is what he calls your *non-communicating self*, a repository of private experience whose meaning consists in its being singularly and inalienably yours. *The artist*, of course, is no different from anyone else in this regard. Winnicott invokes her only because she brings to light the strange simultaneity, common to us all, of the impulses to display and to conceal, *to communicate* and *not to be found*. You want the world to see the singular self you are and to preserve that self from the world's intrusive curiosity and scrutiny.

This is a logical contradiction only if we think of the communicating self as rigidly opposed to the non-communicating self. For Winnicott, one of the lessons of psychoanalytic practice is that you experience true privacy only in and through the presence of another. This paradoxical truth has its roots in infancy.

Try to imagine the intensity and strangeness of a baby's earliest experiences. An avalanche of needs and desires, of sensations and signals assails her from within and without. Lacking the capacity to differentiate her inside from her outside, she has no means of giving form to these perpetual diffusions of pleasure and pain. Hers is a necessarily and radically solitary experience. Yes, observational and neurological research indicates a capacity to distinguish her mother's sensuous properties – voice, smell, skin texture – from those of others. But we shouldn't be too quick to filter this data through the terms of adult consciousness. The capacity of the baby's senses to register different qualities isn't to be confused with the means to distinguish her self from another's.

The baby's ordinary state, says Winnicott, is one of *unintegration* – of relaxed, aimless sensuous and psychic floundering. The task of a caregiver is to *hold* her physically and emotionally through this state, to provide a kind of rudimentary form for the formlessness of the baby's experience. In rocking, stroking, touching and talking to her, a mother gradually and imperceptibly confers the security of a shape on the dizzying obscurity of her baby's world. The more this physical and emotional attentiveness is lacking, the more unintegration is liable to shade into *disintegration*, into a traumatic sense of the absence of any support for her very being, felt as a fall into a bottomless void.

In other words, where the baby's formless experience is invisibly lined by the caregiver's presence, it will strengthen and enrich the self she'll eventually become. But if the caregiver is more distinguished by literal or emotional absence, the self will be correspondingly impoverished and its internal experience, especially at its outer reaches of love and hate, experienced as a mortal danger. A self imperilled in this way will likely find some means of severing itself from its inner life. But this apparent gain in self-preservation is also a terrible loss, severing the self's contact with the unconscious sources of its creativity and curiosity.

To risk the plunge into your own depths, to be in proximity to the unsettling strangeness of your private experience, in short *to be alone*, requires the internalized assurance that you're not alone. *It is only when alone (that is to say in the presence of someone), that the infant can discover his own personal life*, writes Winnicott. A child doesn't fear the dark, Freud had suggested decades earlier in the last of his *Three Essays on the Theory of Sexuality*, so much as its implied depletion of love's presence. The drama of the theory is staged (as it so often is in Freud) in a footnote recalling a three-year-old boy he once heard *calling out in a dark room: 'Auntie, speak to me! I'm frightened because it's so dark.' His aunt answered him: 'What good would that do? You can't see me.' 'That doesn't matter'*, replied the child, *'if anyone speaks, it gets light.'* Thus what he was afraid of was not the dark, but the absence of someone he loved.

There can be few more poignant illustrations of the basic logic of psychoanalytic treatment. It too is an immersion in darkness lighted by the presence of another. On the couch as in the crib, you're *alone (that is to say in the presence of someone)*. In everyday life, the presence of another will often be felt as an intrusion on your privacy. But in the consulting room, it's the very condition of your privacy, of a protected space for emotional and imaginative cultivation, a paradox brought to life in a dream of one of Winnicott's patients, recorded in his essay on the non-communicating self: *A woman patient dreamed: two women friends were customs officers at the place where the woman works. They were going through all the possessions of the patient and her colleagues with absurd care. She then drove a car, by accident, through a pane of glass.*

Having related the dream, patient and analyst tease out a certain triumphalist tone in it: it doesn't matter how deeply they burrow into the contents of my experience, it seems to say, the silent core of me will remain out of reach.

The woman associates to a mother who'd sought to insinuate

herself into her daughter's *secret self*. She remembers a scrapbook she'd kept of favourite poems and sayings, labelled *My private book*, its front page bearing the epigraph, *What a man thinketh in his heart, so is he.* Her mother had betrayed having read it by asking where she got this saying from. *This was bad*, notes Winnicott, *because it meant the mother must have read the book. It would have been alright if the mother had read the book but said nothing.*

Note the subtlety of this detail: the sense of intrusion is located not in the reading of her private book, so much as in the implicit admission of having read it. Reading the book and saying nothing might be dishonest, but at least implies acknowledgement of its privacy, even in the act of violating it. The unattributed quotation, in fact from the Book of Proverbs, intimates the triumphal reproach of the dream: I possess, it says, a concealed emotional and imaginative interior, inaccessible to you my mother as to the customs officers of my dream. The woman shows Winnicott and us that there's a self you nurture invisibly, a self in excess of you, rendering you more than you appear or can make appear.

You might notice a certain ambiguity about both the dream and the scrapbook. There's a wish to withhold the contents of the bag, or the heart, from the sight of others. And yet equally an unmistakable wish for the curiosity and interest of the other. Something about these scenarios repeats the basic paradox of infantile life: the baby wants to be alone, but needs someone to be there to make it possible.

There's a quietly oddball appeal to L., a woman in her twenties. When I open the door to her, I see the robustness of a thoroughbred spliced with the airiness of a pixie. She'll be seeing me five times a week, a fact that seems to register as a kind of physical force in her coiled limbs, her tightly clamped lips as she lies down for the first time. There is, she knows, a delicious promise of cocooned intimacy in the offer of my daily, intent presence. But she doesn't dare enjoy it, liable as it is to shade into a violent sexual threat. *Rape*, writes Winnicott, in one of his essay's more florid passages, *and being eaten by cannibals, these are mere bagatelles as compared with the violation of the self's central core*.

L.'s early life has been played out in the shadow of bloody civil wars, outside and inside her childhood home. She's one of my first patients, a good teacher in so many ways, not least in putting me in such immediate and palpable contact with the hate the presence of a psychoanalyst can induce. I'm offering her a frighteningly ambiguous gift: a presence in which to experience her secret isolation. It's a gift desperately wanted, and potentially terrible for that very reason. *I feel vulnerable, helpless. You're sitting behind me, I can't see you, it's like I'm being trapped. I'm just lying here feeling like a corpse.*

In the weeks that follow, she complains bitterly of attacks, lying in bed at night, of pins and needles in her back, inducing the vertiginous sensation of a fall into a bottomless void. This, her body is letting me know, is how dangerous it feels to be alone. I try not to hear her talk of falling as metaphor. She *is* falling, into the deep of her own self, not daring to imagine that I'm there to catch her, or even to watch with her.

As long as she's compelled to talk, to swim in the treacherously unpredictable currents of need and desire, the couch is anything but restful. She's Jonah and I, if not God, am at least the shipmaster shaking her into consciousness of the storms raging inside her. Dreamless sleep, numb, silent, blank, is the only safe place. She doesn't want contact, with me or anyone else. She's an artist who's abandoned art, a young woman who's abandoned her sexual body.

No sooner does she talk of the things that bring her to life than she falls silent. She wants to make paintings, she tells me one day, *glossy and seductive.* Then she breaks off for a minute, returning to speech with a defiant flatness that drains the room of all the excitement that's just been animating it. *I can't talk about making art, it overwhelms me.* I wait before saying, *As though you're unleashing something that'll undo you.* Another pause. *Just being awake undoes me,* she replies. *Making art or sex, it all makes me feel too awake. Better to slip under the duvet and forget.*

6

'A confessing animal'

My analyst's consulting room, years ago. I've lain down for one of the five weekly sessions of an analysis just weeks old. These first days I've been walking with zealous vigour to every session, powered by a craving for self-discovery. Anxious lest I miss a single second of insight, I arrive with minutes to spare, anticipating my collection from the waiting room with the expectancy of a child scanning the road outside the school gates for his mother's face.

Only today it's not worked out this way. I've arrived under a cloud of confusion and distress, unable to say how it is that I'm fourteen minutes late.

'I was on my way as usual,' I insist to him or to myself, fingertips of my left hand pressed to my knotted forehead, coiled facial muscles enlisted in the breathless, panicky effort of explanation, 'then before I knew it I'd walked in completely the wrong direction. Ten minutes till the session and there I was, miles away, had to run for a bus.' I'm exasperated. I've read Kafka, Camus, Beckett, I know very well nothing makes any sense. But this . . . this doesn't make any sense. 'I left on time, I always leave on time, the last thing I want to do is miss my session.' I doggedly trace and retrace my walk aloud, in the forlorn hope that the explanation will reveal itself somewhere along the path.

But some way into the fourth repetition, I throw my arms down in exasperated concert, the double thud of the couch announcing my defiantly humiliated surrender. 'I don't know, I don't know,' I lament, as though this is the worst admission I could make. Only the ensuing silence reminds me of what I seem to have lost sight of in the course of this tortured monologue – that I'm actually talking to someone, who may well be listening.

From behind me, in a bass tone neither sympathetic nor hostile: 'Where were you going?'

Hope reignites in me. I've read enough Freud to recognize the properly psychoanalytic resonance of this question! I translate to myself swiftly, what was my unconscious wish? I reel off the names of streets, of the tube station I was in front of at the moment I'd realized my error, wondering if the wish is ciphered in some pun or anagram secreted in this pile-up of syllables. Or was I walking towards the real or symbolic site of some unnameable childhood trauma?

'I'm not sure,' I say. 'In my mind, I could've been going to a number of different places.'

A pause, a few seconds. Then, drily: 'Hmm. In any case, not here.'

I'm struck dumb for a moment. Then, just as I'm about to ask him what he means, I burst out laughing. It feels like a moment less of revelation than of possession, or dispossession. I'm laughing hard but don't really know why.

There's a moment where Freud talks about this experience of unexplained laughter as a kind of internal chemical reaction caused by the unexpected intrusion of the unconscious into the waking mind. Something about this clash of registers, he suggests, *appears 'comic' and excites laughter.* A piece of unconscious life your conscious mind has long and painstakingly contrived to keep out suddenly appears in all its naked glory.

Which might help explain the explosion set off in me by my analyst's words. Neither of the traditional metaphors for psycho-analytic investigation – archaeology and detective work, with their intimations of precise forensic inquiry and analysis – applies here. I've been undone not by some intricate reconstruction of a previously obscured childhood event, nor by the anatomizing of an erotic or destructive fantasy, but by a simple and unarguable observation: wherever you were going, it wasn't here.

A simple observation came to condense a range of different meanings. First, apparently I didn't want to come here as much as I thought I did. My commitment to psychoanalysis screens out my hostility to it. I prefer not to hear what my tragi-comic diversion this morning expresses so plainly, but my laughter registers that I've heard it nonetheless. And yet I want to protest: *I* don't want to come here? *Me*, with my fearless curiosity about myself, about analysis? What would possibly make you say I'd want to be somewhere else, other than that I went somewhere else?

Second, analysis will take me where I didn't think I was going. Wherever I imagined my explanations and avowals and speculations were leading, it wasn't here, confronted with my wish to be miles away, to tell analysis and analyst to fuck off, to be spared the ache of self-knowledge. Whatever I find out in analysis will be despite, rather than because of, my conscious efforts. I'm not the intrepid mariner of my inner life, effortlessly navigating its boundless waters, but its hapless passenger, borne and blown by its ferociously unpredictable waves. I don't know where I'm going, least of all when I think I do.

Third, wherever I go in analysis, I take *someone else* with me, someone liable to take command of the ship without me noticing. This, I rightly object, is true outside analysis too – the unconscious is always lurking at the edges, brooding on some mutinous strike. But analysis has the peculiar capacity to draw this someone else, ordinarily concealed in the folds of daily life, occasionally rippling its surface, into undue prominence. My protestations aren't so disingenuous. *I* actually was going to my session. I just didn't twig that where I was going was no longer up to me. Like it, him, her or not, this is my companion, my accompanist, my twin for the duration of analysis and life. Sometimes, *someone else* gets to decide where I go.

I imagined I was there to tell the truth. As though the truth were mine to tell.

What do we talk about when we talk about telling the truth?

Shrink Rap, a properly distressing late-night TV programme broadcast over three years from 2007, offers one authoritative answer. Writers, politicians, actors and comedians subjected themselves to sustained emotional interrogation by clinical psychologist and fellow celebrity Dr Pamela Connolly. It offered the intimacy and discretion of the consulting room, but handily transposed to the glare of the TV studio. It gave us a view of the vulnerable, frightened and besieged inner self ordinarily protected by the celebrity's seamless public persona. And what, after all, could be a more poignantly self-defeating attestation to their vulnerability than their willingness to broadcast it globally?

As a clinical psychologist I have always been fascinated by the inner self, Connolly explained in an online gloss on her show, *but this is the first time such depths have been revealed publicly.* The depths of the inner self publicly revealed – don't we catch a glimpse here of the dream bitterly surrendered with Reverend Hooper's final breath? For this hour at least, the celebrity heart *does not vainly shrink from the eye of his Creator*, nor of his more sublunary creators on the other side of the TV screen, but *shows his inmost heart to his friend* and everyone else. The celebrity's black veil of *luminous perfection*, Connolly assured us, would be raised by her gently penetrating inquiries, to reveal a true face *just as frail, haunted, lonely as the rest of us.*

The echo of the Reverend is neither whimsical nor coincidental, for what Connolly called 'The Theory Behind Shrink Rap' belongs firmly to the religious tradition of truth-telling we commonly call confession, a *use of language*, as the literary theorist and critic Paul de Man writes, *in which the ethical values of good and evil are superseded by values of truth and falsehood*. In the confessional universe, it's never enough merely to believe in the value of truth. Your commitment to truth can be authenticated only by your willingness to share it with any- and everyone. For as long as the confessional principle has prevailed, so has the imperative to write and publish your confession, to have the world bear witness to it. The cameras aren't simply neutral instruments recording the confession, but intrinsic to its very texture. This isn't a private conversation into which a camera has surreptitiously intruded, but a public unveiling of the inner self by the camera.

This version of the truth-telling self was inaugurated by none less than St Augustine (354–430), the North African bishop and pre-eminent theologian of the early Christian period. The *Confessions*, his great narrative of personal revelation and salvation, tracing the Platonic movement of the soul from the shadowy illusions of the cave to the reality of the world outside, tells of a passage from the darkness of life lived in error to the light of life lived in truth. Until it opens itself to the flood of God's light, the hapless soul, stuck in a kind of exitless private hell, stumbles perpetually over obstacles it can't see or feel, condemned to misrecognize lies as truth, stupidity as wisdom, ugliness as beauty.

Nowhere, Augustine tells us, was this state of inner darkness experienced more viscerally than in mourning for the beloved friend of his youth. *I carried my lacerated and bloody soul*, he writes, *when it was unwilling to be carried by me. I found no place where I could put it down.* Grief is the place where you lose sight of yourself, where pain overwhelms your capacity to perceive the world or yourself. *Everything was an object of horror, even light itself.* It's hard to imagine the insidiously voluptuous masochism of grief rendered more vividly. To mourn is to take refuge in the infernal extremities of privacy, where nothing and no one is allowed in for fear of breaking up the total sovereignty of darkness. Staring intently into the consulting-room ceiling, a young man speaks to me of the childhood loss of his mother to disease. 'My grief is so private,' he avows in a disturbingly affectless monotone, 'I can't even reveal it to myself, let alone you.'

When he believed his beloved Joseph dead, Genesis tells us, Jacob *refused to be comforted* – that is, renounced the false relief of the world we share, in deference to the unshareable truth of his private pain. If and when you can finally bear to take your distance from it, grief will show you that your soul, left to its own devices, will retreat ever more deeply and wilfully into the black hole of misprision. *I did not know*, says Augustine, *that the soul needs to be enlightened by light from outside itself, so that it can participate in truth, because it is not itself the nature of truth. You will light my lamp, O Lord. My God you will lighten my darknesses.* This is why you confess, and why you publish – make public, deprivatize – your confession. The Godless soul is a soul abandoned to the dark, to a dense internal fog which renders everything within and without incomprehensible. Grief is unbearable because it registers the loss not only of love but of meaning, of the world's intelligibility. By flooding this void of sense with divine light, confession abolishes the darkness. The tormenting meaninglessness of private pain, assigned its rightful place in the divine order, is redeemed.

Isn't this the effective *Theory Behind Shrink Rap*? To bring the celebrity's private grief, the abject history of traumas, humiliations, failures and rejections concealed by her immaculate façade into public visibility? Instead of festering in shame in the inner chamber of her heart, the celebrity's pain is spoken and witnessed in language intelligible and accessible to herself and everyone else.

But how is psychoanalysis any different? Doesn't it also enjoin the patient to speak and so release the suffering trapped in the recesses of the mind and body? The term 'talking cure', coined in 1880 by the first psychoanalytic patient, Bertha Pappenheim or 'Anna O.', and recorded by her neophyte therapist, Freud's first and short-lived collaborator, Josef Breuer, seems to capture just this intimate link between truth-telling and the restoration of the self. The suffering psyche of the hysteric, suggest Freud and Breuer in 1893, is afflicted by *reminiscences* – that is, by un-processed experiences lodged invisibly in its deepest core, betraying themselves in the form of inexplicable physical symptoms. The hysteric can be delivered from her agonies only by bringing these psychical *foreign bodies* to the surface in the form of speech. *We found*, they report in their so-called 'Preliminary Communication', *that each individual symptom immediately and permanently disappeared when we had succeeded in bringing clearly to light the memory of the event by which it was provoked and in arousing its accompanying affect, and when the patient had described that event in the greatest possible detail and had put the affect into words.*

This seems to describe well enough what Connolly does in her interviews. Steered by her questions and observations, the featured celebrity brings to light memories of traumatic events, arousing the *accompanying affect* of grief, rage, sorrow or shame before *putting the affect into words*. And yet there's a difference: unlike Connolly, Freud and Breuer can't descend into the occulted vaults of their patients' histories assuming they know what they're going to find. This is what Freud discovered when he consented without protest to Emmy's injunction to stop asking her questions and let her tell what she had to say. Don't listen to me, she implies, as though you already know what you're going to hear.

What Connolly refers to as the *true self*, in all its frailty and loneliness, emerges into the light of the TV studio fully formed, ready to laugh, cry and rage on cue. Watch the interviews with Carrie Fisher or Robin Williams and notice the ready compliance with which the *true self* emerges from its hiding place as soon as Connolly starts to coax it into the light. 'You want to see my true self?', the interviewees seem to be saying. 'But of course, here it is'. Early neglect and abuse, promiscuity, addiction, failure, betrayal – there's something disconcertingly reassuring about the readily yielded catalogue of pain and its *accompanying affect*, about its conformity to a familiar script, and above all about the affirmative warmth of Connolly's smile, a kind of mirror to your own gratitude for the pointedly infantile pleasure of hearing exactly the story you asked for. Not for nothing was the show screened late at night. Its appeal is precisely the repetitive gratification of the bedtime story.

Unless, of course, it doesn't quite go according to plan.

I've tried to find online the David Blunkett *Shrink Rap* I remember watching late one night, only to be thwarted at each attempt by a message about copyright exclusion. Perhaps I should take it as a sign. The contents of the discussion, after all, are well beside the point by now. As Freud says of dreams, it's what you remember that matters. And what I remember is something like the stumbling tango of two comically mismatched conversational dancers, each perpetually out of step with the other. Therapy as unintended slapstick. The problem was that Connolly approached the encounter in the spirit of a compact, whereby her interlocutor would tacitly accede to all the premises implicit in her questioning: that your earliest relationships shape your later ones, for example, or that it's important to attend closely to your deepest feelings or that *you are just as frail, haunted, lonely as the rest of us*. What soon became evident was that Blunkett had acceded to nothing, had accepted the invitation to the dance without a thought of learning the steps.

I don't recall much of what he or she said, more the increasingly fraught interchange of vocal tones and facial cues. Connolly's soothing address and wide-eyed concern, met each time by Blunkett's faintly amused breeziness, her sorrowful glance and furrowed brow parried by his genially idiotic grin. Every weapon in her formidable artillery – the respectfully curious question, the helpfully proffered insight, the empathetic hum – was brought to bear on gaining entrance to the sealed fortress of his inner life, only to fall limply against the iron door of his cheery indifference. She ventured some link between his recent personal disasters and his childhood. 'Ah, I see where you're going with that, very clever!' he responded with an indulgent half-chuckle edging towards impatience.

It was then Connolly who became impatient, her tone and expression increasingly reproachful, as though there were something personal in the dismissively unseeing stare he directed past her, in the windy rationalizations he substituted for authentic emotional engagement. She cut across him with compacted, dart-like phrases, the therapist as Paxman, equally intent on ensuring the politician didn't get away with his evasions.

This is the first time such depths have been revealed publicly, Connolly claimed. Was this, then, to be the instructive exception, an object lesson in the perils of emotional dissociation and the refusal of meaningful contact? Yet this was surely the one episode in which the show, in spite of itself, revealed any depths. It showed you that the *true self*, in so far as it's true, doesn't comply with the demand to reveal itself, to perform to and for the world. That, suggests Winnicott, is the function of the false self. The true self, on the contrary, conceals, evades, dissimulates and disguises. The more you seek to draw it out of the dark, the more insistently it will burrow itself into it.

'How do you know a patient is married?' my clinical supervisor abruptly asked me during one of our first meetings. Caught off guard, I stammered in blank anxiety, wondering what trap I was walking into. 'Um, well . . . because . . . she tells me she is?' She paused, noting my confusion in her steady glance, and replied with a half-smile, 'Right. Only because she tells you she is.'

It takes a while to fully absorb the import of that 'only'. It shouldn't be confused with the sceptical caution to trust only what you can verify for yourself, or not to confuse the whole of reality with what one person tells you about it. 'Only' intimates a subtler and more elusive teaching about the strange plane of psychoanalytic listening.

You meet your patient in an enclosed space and time, sealed off to all but the two of you. Neither of you is ever invited to enter the other's life outside this space. Over the days and weeks and years, she speaks of the people and places that fill the time between sessions, her husband for example. You hear of how loving, insensitive, imaginative, dull, predictable, brilliant, incomprehensible, generous, funny, slobbish, desirable and dim-witted he is. Slowly he assumes a real, vivid and intricate existence for you, an existence that has its source not in the world outside, where her husband remains a stranger, but in the space between your two minds. When you hear the words *my husband*, you're referred not to the fleshly being to whom she'll return home, but to an imagined entity forged collaboratively in this room, between what she tells you and what you hear. You know her husband intimately, but only because she tells you.

This is the ambiguous privilege reserved to the psychoanalyst: to inhabit a space located in what Freud called *psychic* as opposed to *external* reality, in the obscurity of private rather than the clarity of public life and language – although this shouldn't be taken to mean that analyst and patient employ a specialized vocabulary.

The fact that psychoanalysis is conducted strictly in ordinary language, explicitly avoiding the jargon of 'frustrated id-wishes' or 'introjection of a bad object', is what renders it uncanny. It brings to light the secret concealed not behind, but in the everyday. It shows up the unsuspected strangeness hidden in the frayed language and perception of daily life. It doesn't need a specialized language to reveal this strangeness – everyday language is more than strange enough.

The language of daily life is tricky as well as strange. It allows, even encourages you to speak and to hear as though words meant what they say and no more. Someone says *my husband* and most of the time whoever's listening will assume that the person designated exists and is bound to the speaker by a marriage contract. You're at a dull work do, caught in some polite exchange with a collegial acquaintance, when a man pulls up beside her. She turns to him and, tenaciously holding her nervily hard bite of a smile, says with a flourish of her upturned palm to his middle, 'This is my husband', who in turn extends his hand to yours, mirroring your lifeless grin. You're in a world of public verities, where the more or less reliable correspondence of word to thing has to be assumed, where the private ambiguities of words have been banished. You take her words as a statement of fact, their truth handily attested to by the physical presence of the very being they designate. You don't listen for irony or bitterness or passion, for the grinding misery or grateful joy or passive resignation her words conceal.

What, after all, are you going to say? 'I sense you wish he weren't?' Who isn't grateful for the essential discretion of words, for their capacity to shield private truths from the intrusions of others, to ensure that sometimes cigars are just cigars and husbands just husbands? Who has yet reached the point of abandoning privacy in favour of a fully transparent life?

Self-preservation dictates that more often than not you treat language as the instrument of the external world that *designates things*, as Blanchot writes, *according to what they mean. This is the way everyone speaks.* But psychoanalysis is nothing if not a space in which you can safely surrender this defensively rigid relationship to your words, where you can listen to them in another dimension.

Perhaps this can help make sense of a seemingly puzzling development in modern psychoanalytic theory. In the course of the 1950s, the British analyst Wilfred Bion published a series of seminal papers exploring the mechanisms of psychotic thinking. Bion was and still is considered a major figure in the tradition associated with the thought of Melanie Klein, and his ideas about psychosis drew heavily on her theories of projective identification, the means by which one self psychically 'throws' the hated and unwanted contents of his mind – greed or envy or cruelty – into the receptacle of another's mind. Without losing interest in this question, Bion began in the early 1960s to reconceive the psychoanalytic enterprise in the light of what might be regarded as a very different and more arcane problem:

how do you represent a clinical session? That is, how do you narrate and describe what took place between analyst and patient?

Why should this be a problem at all? A session is an event like any other. If an analyst wishes to discuss her work with colleagues, can she not simply record as accurately as possible its contents – what was said, the length of the silences, the tone and bodily comportment of the patient, even the inner responses of the analyst? This is how many analysts worked in Bion's time and continue to work today.

Bion felt that this way of representing clinical work fostered a serious misrepresentation of psychoanalysis, distorting its very essence. When you record what a patient says, the words on the page read as though they refer to the external world. A patient says he's married, for example, and on paper this inevitably reads as a reference to his legal and domestic circumstances. But if the analyst in the session listens with an ear attuned only to this publicly verifiable reality, he'll lose access to the singularly private life struggling to be heard inside the patient's words. *The belief*, writes Bion, *that an event belongs to a category of 'events of external reality' leads to confusion and contradiction*. If you drag the meanings of ordinary life and language into the consulting room and let them define what you hear, you lose your ear for psychic reality, for the unconscious currents swirling in the slipstream of the most mundane words.

Disburden yourself of the *penumbra of associations* you carry around outside the consulting room, Bion urges the analyst, and you may hear the patient's reference to his wife rub against your own feeling that your *married patient is unmarried; if so, it means that psycho-analytically his patient* is *unmarried: the emotional reality and the reality based on the supposition of the marriage contract are discrepant*. In other words, the external fact of the patient's marriage may conceal (from himself as much as the analyst) his psychic perception of himself as unmarried.

A certain caution is required here. Psychoanalysis, you'll be relieved to hear, doesn't abolish the external world, as though psychic truth were the only truth worthy of the name. Nor does it plunge you into some interior Bizarro World in which all known reality is inverted. It seeks to show you that your speaking, thinking, acting self lives in more than one dimension, that your experience and the meanings you give it can never be exhausted by the external world, that the experience of being married always exceeds its definitions by civil or religious authorities. The self on display is always haunted by its imperceptible double.

From his earliest publications as a young neurologist researching aphasiac disorders to his late psychoanalytic writings, Freud would return insistently to one of psychology's most intriguing puzzles: how it is that a thought or feeling undergoes a passage from your interior self to its expression in words?

Your mind and body are perpetually subjected to the wordless vagaries of pleasure, pain, need and desire. In *The Ego and the Id*, Freud assigns to these *internal perceptions* the precisely imprecise name of *'something'*. How is it, he asks, that these obscure agitations of *something*, forever murmuring under the surface of consciousness, become sufficiently real to acquire the solidity of a name?

You and I are liable to talk about these *somethings* – sadness, anger, shame, love, hate – as though they had the objective status of stones and trees. And it's true enough that these psychic states can express themselves in the very palpable forms of tears, blushes or flaring nostrils. But no one's likely to confuse such signs with the feelings themselves. You can laugh emptily, cry on cue or simulate orgasms, and so deceive others and even yourself into perceiving an inner state that isn't there. Conversely you can seethe or yearn or despair without anyone around you, or even you perceiving it. I sometimes wonder if this fact, the elemental premise of literature and psychoanalysis alike, ever astonishes us quite as much as it should: *you can hide how you feel*, from others and from yourself.

Evidently it quietly astonished Jane Austen, which may do a lot to account for the spell she cast over me as a sixth-former whose unformed literary enthusiasms had till then run largely to the blokeish pleasures of Orwell and Greene. Wedded to the kind of hardbitten cynicism that comes only with vast inexperience, I felt her unsentimental materialism licensed me to like her.

There's no life, Austen shows us with unsparing clear-sightedness, that escapes the tyrannically grave and petty demands of the external world. Money, class, family, fashion, all the artifices human history has forged to aggravate desire, misery, joy and envy, weave themselves insidiously into the smallest and largest regions of everyday life. In Austen I discovered the famed anatomist of this claustrophobic rule of surfaces, an unforgiving mirror to my anxieties about being, and not being, *handsome, clever, and rich*.

Read in a class of adolescent boys clinging to the life raft of their aggressive, fragile knowingness, *Emma* was a book about the crushing force exerted over human relations by an oppressive, comically intricate system of social codes. Unlike the credulous girl readers of our fantasies, we knew better than to be swept dreamily across the arc of romantic triumph. We saw Austen for the pitiless ironist she was, exposing love as the illusion fostered and co-opted by the institution of marriage to ensure the perpetuation of a class-bound patriarchy. Not that this was why I loved *Emma*, and Emma, which had more to do with perceiving her as the forgiving mirror to my need to know everything and the vulnerable ignorance that need so precariously concealed. Like her, I could convince myself a person was reducible to the outward signs they displayed – a haircut, a favourite band, a shirt collar – as though these talismans could fend off the irreducible terror of living.

Though I should stress I was nothing like Emma, being rather less sensitive to the vibrations of the external world, and rather more so to the dramas raging invisibly in my flesh. Yet I could see the appeal of taking refuge in the shallow verities of the visible, of cutting off from the world bubbling obscurely under your skin and skull, from the turbulence concealed in the polished smiles and casual insults you offered and received.

The passage from *something* to its verbal expression, Freud suggests, is almost alchemically transformative. Translated into words, the spectrally thin substance of private life is suddenly endowed with the density of reality. You say 'I'm sad', or 'I'm married', and these airy phrases are assigned a place among the solid things of worldly life, *as if they came from without*. Words are an insidious ruse in this respect, lulling you into forgetting their origin in interior darkness.

Only in Emma, the *something* of inner experience expires before it reaches conscious expression, consigning her erotic life to the dark. A stranger to herself, numb to the most violent agitations of mind and flesh, she glides in seductively imperious blindness to the man who desires her, then to the man who doesn't and then, most startlingly of all, to the man she desires. Her assured possession of the visible world around her is mirrored in her dispossession by the invisible world within her. Her impassioned ignorance is a window on to the chasm between these worlds.

There's an anxious passage mid-way through the *Confessions* in which Augustine wonders whether the project of public confession might not be doubly self-defeating. On the one hand, why bother confessing to God? It's not as though you can tell him anything he hasn't already heard. *What could be hidden within me, even if I were unwilling to confess it to you?* God's ear is a wiretap secreted in every soul. And what's more, *you hear nothing true from my lips which you have not first told me.* In confessing, you don't tell the truth, you just plagiarize it from God. You wonder if His days can pass in anything other than profound boredom, like some celestial film director riveted forcibly to an eternal loop of his own, badly dubbed movies.

Confessing to your fellow men and women throws up a different set of doubts. How, asks Augustine, do I know the appeal of these *Confessions*, and specifically the revelations of youthful sexual sin, won't be more prurient than pious? *Good people*, he assures himself, *are delighted to hear about the past sins of those who have now shed them. The pleasure is not in the evils as such, but that though they were so once, they are not like that now.* It's difficult to suppress a supercilious analytic 'hmmm' in response to this suggestion that no one would want to read about your murky sexual past for any other motive than the eventual pleasure of your atonement.

If confessing to God is superfluous because he already knows everything about you, confessing to men is superfluous because they know nothing about you, and have no means of guaranteeing you're in earnest. *As I make my confession they wish to learn about my inner self, where they cannot penetrate with eye or ear or mind. Yet although they wish to do that and are ready to believe me, they cannot really have certain knowledge.* This was surely what my supervisor was telling me – your knowledge of the other rests on the fragile support of what she tells you.

The ingenuity of Augustine's solution to this twin problem almost redeems its logical dubiousness. If God knows your confession to be true, he'll ensure its other recipients will too. God's love will open the ears of your fellow human beings, and *those whose ears are opened by love believe me*. God, that is, endows the human recipient of confession with a guarantee of its truth.

But Augustine's solution reads like a hasty patch sewn over the rent he's made in the texture of human relationships by exposing their essential, lonely predicament. To say God knows you better than yourself, that He's the source of human fellowship and trust, is also to intimate a profane world in which you're abandoned to the most meagre and fragile knowledge of yourself and others. Around and within you are infinite imperceptible regions you *cannot penetrate with eye or ear or mind*.

And if you can no longer rely on God to verify the truth of your confession, if you're to resign yourself to the presence of a black veil between you and your own and every other self, do you give up on the aspiration to learn and tell the truth about yourself? Paradoxically, the more the modern secularized world is confronted with the essential obscurity of the self, the greater its rage to hear and see it in its unalloyed truth. Far from being the exclusive preserve of religion, confession has increasingly become a kind of generalized social imperative. *We have*, writes Michel Foucault, *become a singularly confessing society. The confession has spread its effects far and wide . . . one confesses one's crimes, one's sins, one's thoughts and desires, one's illnesses and troubles; one goes about telling, with the greatest precision, whatever is most difficult to tell . . . Western man has become a confessing animal.*

Once the reassuring religious faith that kept our impulse to tell all within the discrete confines of the confessional dissolves, so do the bounds of the booth. They spread inexorably outward to encompass everyone, everywhere. Scandal rags, reality TV, social networking – our insatiable hunger to make and receive confession is forever being offered new ways of feeding itself.

Fiery zealots for inner truth, you and I can't get enough of one another's *crimes, sins, thoughts and desires.*

A *confessing animal*, however, is peculiarly vulnerable to a lie. As Augustine saw, the power and the precariousness of confession derive from the possibility that what you say may not be true, that I have only your word for it. Here is the basic predicament of human relations in the online world. In providing the means for limitless self-revelation, the Internet has become a fecund breeding ground for deception. Would-be lovers serenade one another with seductive illusions about their height, weight, age, beauty, solvency, wit, creativity and kindness. Virtual communities fall prey to every kind of craven fabrication – the young cheerleader sunnily fighting her battle against a rare blood disease, the single mother of twin toddlers rapidly losing her sight – forged out of cynicism, avarice, sadism, attention-seeking, the poignant and lethal tangle of motives in which deceptions are always somehow caught. The confessional impulse is directed in one and the same movement to hearing and telling the truth about ourselves, and to corroding it.

The lasting fascination of confessional interviews and autobiographies derives less from the secrets they reveal than from the intoxicating illusion they give of access to the confessor's most private self. Take Princess Diana's famed interview with Martin Bashir. Long after the details of desperate adulteries and seething resentments have been forgotten, the image of her cocked oval face, radiating doe-eyed vulnerability, will remain. The content of what she said was a sideshow to the real spectacle of her self-exposure.

Something about those iconic still photographs remains unsettling. The more solemnly her face appeals to my trust, the more liable I am to question it, to wonder if I shouldn't mistrust it. One the one hand, she's all-powerful – I have only her word for what she says, leaving me wide open to deceit, manipulation and seduction. But she's also poignantly defenceless – if her word is all I have, then it's also all she has, and as such can as easily be spurned and rejected as believed. If you won't believe me, her face implores, I'll be left abandoned without hope. This is the peculiar ambiguity of that image, its capacity to convey raw emotional exposure and consummate media con-artistry at once. And there's no mileage in trying to work out which it 'really' is. As soon as you put the private life on display, the clear distinction between honesty and dishonesty, revelation and dissimulation, dissolves.

Set out to tell the whole truth and you'll find yourself haplessly snared in lies, a predicament that's hardly specific to our age of electronic self-exposure. You find it running through the pages of the first great tell-all celebrity autobiography, the one that sets the terms of the genre: the *Confessions* of Jean-Jacques Rousseau.

The *Confessions*, Rousseau announces in his prefatory note, *is the only portrait of a man, painted exactly according to nature and all its truth, that exists and will probably ever exist.* And in that first sentence, he performs the self-defeating paradox of confession: you always say more and less than you intend. More in that his claim to infallible self-knowledge is immediately contradicted by its hubristic lack of self-awareness, calling his trustworthiness immediately into question. And less, for essentially the same reason – if you're not in possession of the entire contents of your inner self, you can't hope to put them on display without something, probably most things, remaining behind.

I have concealed nothing that was bad, Rousseau nonetheless claims in his opening address to the *Supreme Judge*, *and added nothing that was good . . . I have disclosed my innermost self as you alone know it to be.* No Augustinian humility here, then, no insistence on the chasm between God's infallible and your own hopelessly frail knowledge of your self. Rousseau's capacity to see everything but his own blind spots is what makes the book so infuriating and so deliriously funny.

It's hard to read the *Confessions* without hearing the great adolescent refrain of our time: too much information. *I know of course*, writes Rousseau, *that the reader does not need to know these things; it is I who need to tell them.* Too right! you respond, squinting in delirious horror through the gaps between your fingers as he regales you with his adventures in masturbation and flashing, his abject erotic failures, public embarrassments, failures of nerve, unveiling the shabby, creepy, self-serving, chronically insecure self you work so hard to keep from the eyes of the world, not least your own.

You can't read this chronicle of personal weakness without getting caught in the very shame it exhibits so shamelessly. In exposing himself to you, flashing his private life, he exposes you too, brings you up against your voyeurism, your intrusive and sadistic pleasure in the suffering of his naked self. It's all too much, above all because you can't get enough of it.

But it's shaming also in its peculiar inversion of shame: the more Rousseau abases, the more he ennobles himself, makes you feel something of a coward in clinging mean-mindedly to your own secrets. The real aim of the *Confessions*, he insists, isn't to gratify the exhibitionist he is but to fulfil the highest ambition of the philosopher he is, to attain truth itself. And if truth lies within the soul, the soul must be turned inside out for all to see. *But the undertaking I have embarked on, to reveal myself to him* [the reader] *in my entirety, requires that nothing about me should remain hidden or obscure; I must be continually present to his gaze; he must follow me into all the aberrations of my heart, into every recess of my life.* Yet for all his determination to make himself fully transparent to you, Rousseau is always tormentedly aware of all the hidden places into which truth will withdraw before it lets you get hold of it. After all, one of the prime motives for his confession is the predilection of his younger self to lie.

His *one fear in this whole undertaking*, he goes on to say, *is not that I might say too much or tell lies, but that I might not say everything and so conceal some truths*. What fear could be better founded? Confession offers only one guarantee: that you won't say everything and you'll conceal some truths – as famously and excruciatingly illustrated by his recollection of a *crime* perpetrated during his time as a young footman in the house of Mme de Vercellis of Turin.

Caught by the head of household staff with a ribbon he's stolen from the chambermaid, the stammering, blushing little Rousseau tells him a young cook named Marion gave it to him. An inquiry swiftly follows, attended by a large crowd before which he repeats his accusation *shamelessly* to Marion herself. Bewildered, the sweet and virtuous girl *denied the charge . . . remonstrated with me, urged me to recollect myself and not to bring disgrace upon an innocent girl who had never done me any harm*. But Rousseau, persistent in his *infernal wickedness*, fends off her tearful pleas, resulting in her dismissal and consignment to a life he masochistically fantasizes as one of *wretchedness and destitution*.

Owning up to this little piece of infamy is hard enough, but doesn't the real test of confessional integrity lie in calling yourself to account, in telling why you did it? *Surely*, he pleads, *no one could think that I have in any way sought to mitigate the infamy of my crime. But I would not be fulfilling the purpose of my book if I did not at the same time reveal my innermost feelings, and if I were afraid to* **excuse** *myself, even where the truth of the matter calls for it*. Confessing to what you've done is important, but only as the preliminary to the real substance of confession, the revelation of the soul.

Perhaps this is why Rousseau needs to equate his own knowledge of his inner self with God's. Because, as we say, God knows what you're thinking and feeling when you do such awful things. Rousseau's been haunted by his hitherto secret crime for forty years only because he can't know what possessed him to do it, can't claim some pseudo-divine access to his own unconscious. You feel the urge to confess deeds and impulses where they exceed the limits of your understanding, where you're no longer able to recognize yourself in them. To confess something is also to confess your incomprehension before it, whereas once you claim to comprehend it, you have, as Rousseau more or less says, *excused* yourself.

The second stage of confession, explaining what you did, is always in danger of annulling the first stage, simply describing what you did. Certainly this is what happens when Rousseau tries to reveal his motives for accusing Marion. *I have never*, he declares, *been less motivated by malice than at this cruel moment.* On the contrary, his intention had been to give the ribbon to Marion herself, and this is the one secret that no amount of guilt or remorse could induce him to confess. The exposure of his crime could be borne; the exposure of his fondness couldn't. *It was not that I was afraid of being punished but that I was afraid of being put to shame; and I feared shame more than death, more than crime, more than anything in the world.*

And with this fear of shame, Rousseau is led to a rather more forgiving view of his own sin. *Real wickedness is even more criminal in a young person than in an adult, but what is merely weakness is much less so, and my offence, when it comes down to it, was little more.* In the space of a few pages, we've been carried from the tormented confession of an infamous crime to the effective exoneration of a moment's weakness.

It's tempting at this point to resort to moralizing accusations against Rousseau's disingenuousness, his shamelessly self-serving efforts to mollify and manipulate his readers' imagined outrage, as though for all his protests of youthful weakness, you *see through* him, you know what *really* motivated him. But perhaps this is to miss what his blatantly self-contradictory movement from violent remorse to brazen special pleading has to teach us. Might this self-contradiction be a clue to what Rousseau means by his commitment to *say everything*? To say everything isn't to arrive at the definitive truth of your inner self, but to expose it as double, both you and *someone else*, unimaginably courageous and unspeakably cowardly, honest and dishonest to a fault. Is Rousseau to be commended for his unstinting devotion to truth, or derided for his efforts to delude his readers and himself alike? Yes.

In literature, writes Blanchot, *deceit and mystification are not only inevitable but constitute the writer's honesty.* And not just in literature. In confessing, on paper or in speech, what you end up bringing to light is just how much you remain in the dark. You rightly decry the Internet scammer's deceptions, the invented identities, stories and needs, their cynical assault on the trust, vulnerability and generosity of others. But could your indignation at such gross deceptions be a way of screening out the deceit at the heart of all human relations? The Internet only makes plain the disturbing truth of what happens as soon as someone enters into relation with himself or another, for the simple reason that all such relations involve *someone else*. What Rousseau shows you with such unwitting clarity is that you're devious in spite of your irreproachable honesty, in spite of your determined efforts to *say everything*, in spite of your willingness, as *X Factor* contestants like to put it, to *just be myself*.

In the first volume of his *History of Sexuality*, Michel Foucault portrays the consulting room as a wily modern incarnation of the confession booth. He's certainly not the first to notice the likeness in this outpouring of darkest secrets to an unseen other. But the differences, he suggests, are just as instructive. In the booth, the guilty party is the knowing bearer of his sins. On the couch, on the other hand, the patient is posited as ignorant of his sins, now thought of as secret wishes. Psychoanalysis posits sex as *the fragment of darkness that we each carry within us . . . a universal secret . . . a fear that never ends*.

In fact, Foucault implies, this universal mystery is more like a mystification, the real mystery of sex being that there is none, other than that which obscurantist churchmen and shrinks insist on ascribing to it. This projection of sex as an impenetrable secret needing careful and patient decipherment by an expert who then decides and controls its 'real' meaning is only an intricate ruse of *power*, argues Foucault, to maintain its grip on souls and bodies alike.

In psychoanalysis, says Foucault, confession is now split into two stages corresponding to its two participants. In the first, the patient presents the truth *incomplete, blind to itself*. In the second, the analyst returns it deciphered and *wholly formed*.

It's hard not to notice that Foucault's critique, for all its sophistication, rests on one of the crudest popular caricatures of psychoanalysis: that it reveals what you *really* mean, who you *really* are, what's *really* going on in your innermost self. You may appear reasonable, continent, ethical, peaceable, coherent, but you're *really*, if you just let me show you, mad, perverse, corrupt, cruel and chaotic. The return of my party friend's fantasy: you can see through me.

What's missed by this fantasy is that psychoanalysis doesn't see you as *really* any one thing, but as irreducibly double. It can't give you back to yourself *wholly formed* for the simple reason that you're not wholly formed. You are yourself and *someone else*, equally the one who says yes and the one who says no to the bubbling cauldron of excess simmering in you. This is the paradoxical meaning of being a singular self. Where does Rousseau's confession fall apart, lose all plausibility and, in the strict and ordinary sense of the word, integrity? Where he tries to tell you what was 'really' on his mind.

In 1998, the British artist Gillian Wearing threatened (though didn't finally pursue) legal action against the advertising agency BMP DDB for plagiarizing her 1992–3 photographic series *Signs that Say What You Want Them to Say and Not Signs that Say What Someone Else Wants You to Say*. Wearing's now iconic images show individuals she has stopped in the street face to camera, holding up a sheet of white paper bearing the hasty black scrawl of the first thought they'd had when she asked them.

The series' most famous image depicts a young man in a navy business suit, his half-smile at once blunt and apologetic, quizzical and defended, his self-possession betrayed by the shiny brow eating into his brittle strawberry-blond hairline, by the cheap metal lanyard, bearing the laminated ID card concealed in his jacket, cutting across his tie. I'M DESPERATE, his sign announces.

Then there's the young black police officer standing at the edge of a sunlit Covent Garden, in the heels-clicked, toes-out pose of a secretly aspiring clown, eyes concealed in the shadow of his bobby's hat, lips pulled back over exposed teeth suspended between laughter and fear, fingertips daintily pinching by its top corners a sign calling for HELP. Or the attractive young woman, a few strands of her auburn fringe set free from her tight centre parting, leaning louchely against the iron railings, long manicured fingers dangling from beneath her coolly ironic gaze the words MY GRIP ON LIFE IS RATHER LOOSE!

The TV ad for the VW Golf was a montage of similar images. SENSITIVE, reads the sign of a snarling nightclub bouncer, SEX, CHOCOLATE, CHOCOLATE, SEX, proclaims an impassively staring middle-aged female stood in front of a carload of weekly shopping. But the charge of plagiarism, for all its evident plausibility, misses how Wearing's original project is turned by its commercial appropriation into something entirely different.

Most obviously, the signs no longer *say what you want them to say*. They aren't spontaneous responses to an invitation to say whatever comes to mind, but the crafted contrivances of copywriters. They're held not by their authors but by actors, who thereby say precisely *what someone else wants you to say*.

And these are more than descriptive differences. They point to two quite opposed conceptions of the confessional impulse. The VW conception is cutely condensed in its slogan: *Sometimes what you see isn't all you get*. Confession, in this version, reveals who you *really* are, lifts the carefully manicured lid off your secret self. Bruisers who are really sensitive, housewives who are really hedonists.

Encountering Wearing's work over the years, you can't but notice her recurring obsession with the confessional scenario. Over and again, she plays on the disjunction between the manifest self and its private life. But look carefully and you find that her work narrowly avoids the fall into easy truism only because *what you see* isn't crudely opposed to *what you get*.

Wearing spoke of her desperate young suit as being first startled then angered at confronting his own words, handing the sign back to the artist and abruptly walking away. The confession shocks its own speaker, as though it came from *someone else*, a hostile internal assailant from whom he then has to escape. This isn't the private life you knowingly clutch to yourself, a secret possession you keep locked in your internal safe. Your grip on it is rather looser. To *say what you want to say* isn't to reveal who you really are as opposed to who you pretend to be, to lift the black veil and finally expose the true face it conceals. Wearing's images are powerful only because they clarify nothing about their subjects, because each face only exacerbates the strangeness and impenetrability of each sign, and each sign does the same in reverse.

'Just say whatever comes to mind.'

At the nervy threshold of a first psychoanalytic encounter, as the new patient and I start to contemplate what we've got ourselves into, I'll offer this telescopic statement of Freud's *fundamental rule* – the very invitation Wearing offered to her sign-bearers. I try to be as clear and economical as possible, to avoid any gratuitous ambiguity or confusion.

And yet more often than not, the invitation is fed back to me weeks or months or years later, always with some subtle but decisive tweak. *You want me to tell you everything.* Or *I know it's wrong to hold anything back.* Or *I realize I'm supposed to be totally honest here.*

If you've experienced analysis, you'll know how difficult it is to avoid getting caught in this fantasy of what your analyst wants. His offer to receive whatever it is *you want to say* always somehow morphs into the demand to *say what someone else*, the persecutory bastard hovering behind you, *wants you to say*, namely *everything*. Rousseau's imperative becomes your own: *nothing about me should remain hidden or obscure.* All that's required to eliminate this obscurity, he and you imagine, is that you *say everything*. But of course you can't say everything, because you don't know everything, you know the tiniest, most fragile fragment of everything, if that. And if you could say everything, if confession could fulfil its highest aspiration to bring to light all in you that's hidden, what then? Would you feel complete, able to rest secure in your perfect self-knowledge? Or would that be the very point you'd say, *I'm desperate. Help.*

7

'A dark and truncated language'

A Friday in winter. I'm ten, more or less, hugging to myself the knowledge that for a sliver of this hour after dusk I can prowl downstairs undisturbed, willing the fragrant steam of showers, the lure of mirrors and wardrobes, indeed all the narcissistic demands and desires that govern life upstairs, to guard my solitude a bit longer.

I'm suspended in that short interlude before the onset of adolescence and the rage it brings against the world's laughable inadequacy in the face of my needs, before the experience of my body as a troubling and elusive enemy. Soon enough, solitude will feel very different from this idyll of contented hedonism, from the spring of the carpet under my feet, the yellow haze of the hall lights, the caress of my flannel shirt, the wisps of roasting chicken and stewing white beans curling voluptuously under my nostrils. Soon enough, the world will cease to give itself to me in such reassuringly known form.

None of which I'm aware of as I stroll into the dining room and take a turn round the long glass table crowned with old lace, china, silver, crystal, a joyous and melancholy image of the mute perfectibility of things before human noise and use come to soil them.

My eye falls on a gap in the middle of the fitted bookcase housing the twenty-six hefty volumes of the *Encyclopaedia Judaica*. The missing volume rests open on the sideboard below, its heavy black and cream double page, ordinarily so dreary, suddenly a Wonderland siren call: READ ME. I walk over and alight on the single word at the head of the congested sprawl of print and grainy images: HOLOCAUST.

Not an unfamiliar word, this one, a word that has quietly stalked me for as long as I can remember, a word which elders round tables gingerly whisper and indignantly shout, intimating an evil that at once underlines and reproaches the state of prosperity I so unthinkingly enjoy. Hitler, camps, Germany, six million – the starts of uncomprehending fright these phrases induce don't provoke me, as they might other kids, into deeper curiosity. They enforce the message implicit in the adults' pained gravity of tone: you don't want to know.

And I don't, not even now. I wouldn't have chosen to read these pages if they hadn't intruded themselves into my transient idyll, if they hadn't tricked me into mistaking them for part of the romance of the scene. A few lines in, it's already too late. I've fallen deep into this infernal rabbit hole, and there's no scrabbling back up.

I scan randomly, only to be afflicted by the capacity of the worst horrors, as though raising themselves vindictively from the page, to find me. The hyena smiles of the SS officers in the central synagogue aisle, enjoining rows of bare-skulled men to intone prayerfully, heads lowered, *Yes, we are truly filthy people*, or menacing the prone heads of Jews scrubbing the pavement with toothbrushes under the gaze of huddled onlookers. A hollow-eyed man on his knees, staring into the void ahead waiting for the rifle bullet that will send him to the top of the human landfill piled below.

I'm soon snared in the eyewitness account of a man placing his arm around his son's shoulder and pointing to the starry sky as they wait their turn to be shot. I see an image, or rather feel a vacuum irresistibly swallowing the contents of mind and world, leaving nothing but itself and my eye, the pitiful husk of my near-cancelled senses.

The sideways profile of a line of naked women, some holding naked infants, queuing patiently for their own massacre by Ukrainian police, the caption says. You can see one of the children clearly, a curly-headed girl of around two, buttocks resting nonchalantly on her mother's forearm, quizzically extending her curled index finger into the middle distance. My perception is just sufficiently intact to note that these women aren't emaciated, like so many of their counterparts on adjacent pages. Their flesh and hair are no less full than those of the women I glimpse sneakily at the local pool.

For a moment both imperceptible and eternal, it's as though air, gravity and light, the invisible supports on which the world's and my existence rests, have been suspended. My limbs, skin, sense organs, minutes ago an integrated radar for all the textures of reality, have abruptly dropped off, leaving me stranded in a night that is less the opposite than the permanent eclipse of day. These blurry monochrome smudges, obscene in the guileless fraudulence with which they bring these women and children alive, are the end of the world.

I take a breath and slam shut the volume. The room is back in focus. My sudden and ruthless determination to continue as though nothing has happened slightly shocks me. Without any need to formulate to myself the reasons, I know that I can't betray my distress, can't solicit consolation or comfort. The past few minutes will have to be, have already been, permanently excised from the evening's narrative, shunted out of sight.

Blanchot: *The disaster ruins everything, all the while leaving everything intact.* When I came across this sentence twenty years later, I was immediately transported to that evening, to the enigmatically dry-eyed assurance with which I straight away recovered my life of overfed privilege. Perhaps the darkness I'd plunged into during those moments cast just enough light on the ravaged state of my speech to enable me to know, with perfect clarity, that I couldn't share the experience. Understanding nothing, I understood my capacities of speech and perception had been ruined in the blink of an eye. Those naked bodies would have to be sent somewhere too private even for me to reach, somewhere immeasurably distant from the world above, where I would continue to live and where everything would be left intact.

You were born prematurely.

Sentient life began for you in a vessel precisely adapted to your needs, in which food, warmth and shelter were provided from the first with unbroken reliability and constancy, ensuring you registered neither the need of them nor the possibility of their loss. If you expanded, space expanded with you. You were God, to all intents and purposes, the centre of an integral, self-sufficient universe without beginning or end. Profoundly attuned to the syncopated flow of the world's blood and breath, you took the endlessly variegated transmissions of one voice, and even the more tinny and sporadic emanations of other voices, for discrete parts of the music you alone composed, played and conducted.

Perhaps this fantasy of intra-uterine life is simplistic and presumptuous. But its appeal lies in the light it sheds by contrast with the rude shock of birth. Forcibly ejected from your own universe, birth reveals you to yourself for the first time, and incomprehensibly, as a thing in a world of other things, a mere part you'd been cruelly allowed to take for the whole. Your changeless world has disappeared and given way to this unrelenting barrage of disturbances, interruptions and surprises, each diffused across your skin, musculature and internal organs, each reverberating formlessly in your formless mind.

Displaced from the centre of your own story, you find yourself consigned to total dependence, unable to procure for yourself the basic means of survival, or to attend to your own bodily needs and demands. You first encounter the world in a state of profound biological unreadiness and psychical incomprehension. This comprehensive humiliation, the inaugural condition of every human life, is what Jean Laplanche calls *the fundamental anthropological situation*.

Freud's term for this state is pithier, if less precise: *helplessness*. This, you could say, is the organizing concept of his fascinatingly disorganized late essay of 1926, *Inhibitions, Symptoms and Anxiety*. Here Freud famously revises his first theory of anxiety, which posited that stimuli coming from without and within the human organism generated a dangerously pleasurable flow of exciting wishes and impulses, which the psyche defended itself against by repressing them. Repression, that is, was the psychic magic wand which transforms libidinal energy into anxiety, such that what you most wanted becomes what you most fear.

Could it be, Freud wonders in 1926, that this ingenious theory, in the time-honoured manner of ingenious theories, missed a more obvious source of anxiety? Perhaps the problem was that he'd been observing anxiety through the lens of a clinician inquiring into the neuroses, guided by the question 'Why would you be anxious?' Whereas if you observe anxiety through the lens of the universal experiences of birth and early infancy, you might be more likely to ask yourself the opposite question

– 'Why wouldn't you be anxious?' Looked at from this angle, suggests Freud, *anxiety is seen to be a product of the infant's mental helplessness which is a natural counterpart of its biological helplessness.* Anxiety isn't, in other words, a derivative of a more primary state of mind, but an essential condition and inescapable destiny.

Habituated to thinking of yourself as master in your own house, you're apt to forget that you start life feeling rather more like a stranger to it, that your body, your psyche and the world around you are first felt as inexhaustible sources of danger. Hunger and your mother's absence warn you that the gratifications of food and love are liable to be lost; the restriction, obstruction and even the punishment of your wishes and impulses then bring home the perils of desire; and later still you internalize this punitive response to your own desire in the form of what Freud calls a super-ego. Although associated with earlier and later stages of infancy and childhood, these layers of anxiety continue to operate alongside and interact with one another into adolescence and adulthood. Life will be forever haunted by the psychic and physical helplessness into which you're born, and which you're never really allowed to surpass. The infant you'll always be never lets you forget how much you have to be anxious about, how often and easily your experience can exceed your capacity to master it.

Perhaps the real danger, at least in the first instance, isn't so much helplessness as the knowledge of helplessness. A mother's role, according to Winnicott, isn't merely to give her child the bodily support and sustenance he can't provide himself, but to spare him the psychic shock of perceiving his total dependence. The earliest stages of human life, he suggests, demand the kind of care that will restore to the child his fantasized place at the centre of the world, a kind of recreation of the uterus's function of total adaptation. *The mother, at the beginning, by an almost 100 per cent adaptation affords the infant the opportunity for the illusion that the breast is part of the infant. It is, as it were, under the baby's magical control . . . Omnipotence is nearly a fact of experience.*

Cry and you're held, soothed and fed. If that interval is sufficiently short, if at the very moment you signal your distress its remedy appears, it will nourish your illusion that whatever you lack you can immediately supply. *The mother*, writes Winnicott, *places the actual breast just there where the infant is ready to create, and at the right moment.* Mother and baby collaborate, in other words, in a kind of magical inversion of reality whereby his helplessness is transformed into omnipotence.

The baby's care after this initial phase of magic involves the delicate and complex task of dispelling this illusion, of introducing him in small but steadily increasing doses to the truth of his dependence and vulnerability. But if a mother is, in Winnicott's celebrated phrase, 'good enough', this disillusion will never be total. Your unconscious will quietly preserve the omnipotence your conscious mind dutifully renounces, and with it the possibility of creative life.

There is no such thing as a baby, Winnicott famously declared, only *a baby and someone. A baby cannot exist alone, but is always part of a relationship.* Helplessness can't be isolated from the care which relieves it. Few images condense more potently the terror of helplessness than an abandoned baby. Winnicott goes so far as to say *there is no such thing* – that the very possibility of a baby abandoned to itself would expose the precarious nakedness of human life to a degree that renders it literally unimaginable, inadmissible to mind or world. But, you might object, it happens – cruelty and neglect and impoverishment ensure that babies, along with human beings of all ages, are all the time and everywhere abandoned. As Job and Lear and the queuing Ukrainian Jewish women remind us, suffering finds its outermost limit in this experience of unrelieved helplessness. The victim of torture or genocide is coerced into the psychic state of the infant *existing alone*, made to suffer the fate whose possibility Winnicott can't even bring himself to imagine. Which is only to say how often the imagination is unequal to what can happen.

Life is not free of its forms. This is one of the more gnomic of the 'Adagia', a late collection of aphorisms by Wallace Stevens. Stevens seems to suggest that life can't be conceived in isolation from the languages, relationships, communities and cultures in which it's embedded. Or, as the cloying lyric from the *Cheers* theme has it, *You want to go where everybody knows your name*. You need to mean something to a world of others, to have a specified place in what the French analyst Jacques Lacan called the symbolic order. As Darian Leader shows in *What Is Madness?*, it's above all the sense of a sustained place in this order that can make the difference between a latent and a full-blown psychosis. The ultimate psychic catastrophe is to drop out of the network and experience a world where nobody knows your name, where you have no place in a shared universe.

A private life is made possible only by the protective shield of a public persona. In order to nurture itself, the self needs the assurance that its interior can hide undisturbed behind its external face. As Winnicott showed us, the very worst psychic catastrophe is the penetration of this private, non-communicating self. When Reverend Hooper dons his black veil, one of its more quietly pernicious effects is to insinuate into his congregants a feeling of incessant persecutory intrusion: *Each member of the congregation felt as if the preacher had crept upon them, behind his awful veil, and discovered their hoarded iniquity of deed or thought*. The public persona severed from its interior is empty; but the private life deprived of an external guise is blind, and terrifyingly so. The gaze of the minister's black veil is felt by each of his congregation as the pitiless exposure of their deepest self in all its formless chaos. To experience life dissociated from its forms is to be rendered anonymous, literally faceless.

Perhaps it was in exposing this original helplessness that the queue of naked women burned a hole in the inner lining of my ten-year-old self. For those few moments the image stared at me, there was no recourse to the ordinary reflexes of sadness or anger, certainly not to curiosity. How could they have been so compliant with their own destruction? How could they have surrendered on demand the dignity of body and soul? But these stupid questions, as evasive as they were impertinent, were vain attempts to draw the scene into the ambit of recognizable human motives and responses, to leapfrog the violent shock of seeing what human beings look like when stripped of the forms that make life worthy of the name. You can ask why the victims didn't fight or resist or flee only by wilfully ignoring the primary aim of all political terror – to dispossess its victims of those very resources, to return them to the state of helplessness.

As the Holocaust survivor Jean Améry shows with grim sobriety in his seminal essay on the subject, the final aim of torture is to strip human life of its forms. Among the innumerable methods human history has forged of stripping the private self of its protections, torture has proved one of the most durable and brutally efficient. Recounting his interrogation by an SS lieutenant in the Belgian political prison of Breendonk, Améry speaks of the torturer's total and unconstrained sovereignty over his victim. *Torture*, writes Améry, *becomes the total inversion of the social world*. In the *social world*, each individual is bound by a tacit contract to *bridle the desire of the ego to expand* in order to safeguard their own and others' continued right to life.

Torture abolishes this contract. With his very first blow, the torturer inflicts not only physical shock, but an immediate and traumatic loss of trust in the world. *The expectation of help*, writes Améry, *is as much a constitutional psychic element as is the struggle for existence.* When the child calls for his mother, the patient for his doctor, even the wounded soldier for the ambulance, the anxiety and pain are supported and relieved by the expectation of help. What distinguishes torture from other forms of suffering, in other words, is its annulment of this expectation, and with it the recreation of the state of infantile helplessness, now radically shorn of the protective illusion of omnipotence. Deprived of the psychic structure to contain his experience, the torture victim is not only abandoned to bodily pain but reduced to it, *only a body, and nothing else beside that.* Pain becomes interminable because irredeemably meaningless, without any place in the victim's symbolic world. *Physical pain*, writes Elaine Scarry, *does not simply resist language but actively destroys it, bringing about an immediate reversion to a state anterior to language, to the sounds and cries a human being makes before language is learned.*

The pain was what it was, writes Améry. *Beyond that there is nothing to say.* In torture, the self is dragged forcibly into this zone of expressive nothingness, expelled from the world of shared, communicable meanings and abandoned to an entirely private inner existence. The infant in the more or less reliable care of a parent is, writes Winnicott, *alone (that is to say in the presence of someone).* The victim of torture finds herself back in the position of that infant – helpless, alone, only now in the presence of less than no one. True, the torturer is there. But in the acts of inflicting and impassively witnessing his victim's pain and of denying it the relief for which it screams out, in consciously inverting the role of carer, the torturer becomes an obscene parody of *the presence of someone*, the annulment rather than affirmation of human solidarity.

Perhaps this is why the imperative to preserve the voice of human solidarity is so audible in the writings of some of the most authoritative witnesses and victims of atrocity, notably Primo Levi. *We must not write as if we were living alone*, he writes in a short essay called 'On Obscure Writing'. This sombre pronouncement at once moves and unnerves me, stirring up a cloud of nameless anxieties. Why not, I want to respond, what will happen if we do?

As Levi sees it, to write as if you were alone, out of the opaque language of your private self rather than the enlightened language of common perception, is to risk delivering yourself over to a state of helpless, wordless incomprehension, or, to recall Scarry's words, *to the sounds and cries a human being makes before language is learned*.

Levi's essay is a caution to his fellow writers against this kind of descent into obscurity, and an appeal to preserve the humanist project of shared understanding. Taken out of the context of Levi's traumatized life, its prescriptions against writing that is anything less than fully transparent and comprehensible seem peculiarly naïve and parochial. I still find myself bristling at its presumption to know what readers want and need from books. Yet something in me, perhaps the ten-year-old I continue to be, feels a visceral solidarity with it.

A barely concealed rage bubbles under the genial surface of the essay, the target of which he calls *the language of the heart*, the voice speaking out of the dark interior of private life. The language of the heart isn't the ordinary language in which we all recognize ourselves. In fact, *it isn't a language at all, or at most a vernacular, an argot, if not an individual invention*. In other words, it is an idiom, the expressive medium of the singular self, and as such *capricious, contaminated, and as unstable as fashion*.

Because it's a singular rather than universal mode of expression, the language of the heart inflicts on its reader the humiliation of incomprehension. Notwithstanding Levi's opening proviso that *a book or a story . . . is essentially an inert and innocuous object*, books written in this pseudo-language are personified by him as effective torturers, sadistically lording themselves over their reader-victims, who suffocate helplessly in the airless hold of non-meaning. Imposing *labour, anguish, or boredom on his readers*, the obscure writer is at best a *discourteous*, at worst a *wicked* person.

There are times, Levi concedes, when obscurity is the effect less of cruelty than of irreparable damage. He cites his contemporary, the German-language Romanian Jewish poet Paul Celan, who writes like Levi himself out of the shadows of *German slaughter*. For Levi, Celan's lyric obscurity must be ascribed neither to contempt nor to ineptitude, but to *the obscurity of his fate and his generation*, which *grows ever denser around the reader, gripping him as an ice-cold iron vise, from the raw lucidity of* **Death Fugue** *(1945) to the atrocious chaos without a glimmer of light of his last compositions.*

Celan, Levi concludes, is less to be *imitated* than *pitied* as one stripped of the faculty of communicative language and left with its exhausted husk, *a dark and truncated language like that of a person who is about to die and is alone, as we all will be at the point of death.*

Reading these lines splits me in two. On one side sits the adult reader in awe of the bleak, godforsaken sublimity of Celan's poems, a little affronted by Levi's bad faith in presenting pity, the most subtly violent of insults, as empathy. On the other sits the ten-year-old who wants the protection of Levi's faith in a fundament of human rationality, who intuits that only shutting the book will preserve him from sinking into a hermetic silence from which there's no return. I have to remind myself that Levi witnessed the living dead not from the comfort of a centrally heated dining room thirty-six years later, but as their companion in cold, hunger and disease, in unrelenting bodily and psychic violation.

And yet, I recall that queue of naked women, and the suffocating sense of helplessness they evoked in me, and feel the terrible conviction that helplessness is the ruin and mockery of any common language. It's precisely because I recognize Levi's visceral fear of writing as if alone, of being sealed in a language only its speaker can hear, an indecipherable language of howls and tears, that I feel awed gratitude rather than pity for Celan's poetry. In Celan, the voice abandoned to its own mute helplessness somehow, impossibly, speaks meaningfully. *Language*, he writes in a celebrated essay, *in spite of everything . . . remained secure against loss . . . It went through. It gave me no words for what was happening, but went through it. Went through and could resurface, 'enriched' by it all.*

A wide-eyed smile, broad yet tight-lipped, as he rises from the waiting-room chair carrying the same distressed brown leather bag and crosses the consulting-room threshold, his raised jaw signalling purpose and doubt at once. So reliably and ritually changeless is F.'s movement into the analytic space, I sometimes feel I could break it down with the minute precision of a Muybridge sequence.

There's a moment preceding the smile, so fleeting I might just have hallucinated it, when the startled, quietly accusatory eyes of a very young baby stare out from the crow's-footed sockets; a disconcerting and needful reminder that he has not somehow been spared the universal predicament of infancy.

I'm grateful to my unconscious for perceiving this and infusing me with a tenderness for the baby F. once was. It calms my momentary irritability with the man, and makes the smallest of cracks in his impermeable wall of geniality. F. is all proportion, an apparent stranger to bodily or emotional excess, from the near-fleshless skin stretched tight across his compact frame to the even flow of his calibrated speech, syncopated by a chuckle that assures us both we needn't take him or his suffering too seriously.

I don't mean to imply he's insipid, or that there's any shortage of turbulence or pain or complexity in the story he tells. But these qualities are less experienced than spoken about, much as you'd speak about the Crimea or Chinese calligraphy, or any other subject that might arouse your distant fascination. F.'s mournful, angry soul has become for him the set text of a lively scholarly seminar in which he and I are equally diligent, equally curious participants. As his assessor, you'd praise his careful argumentation and thorough background reading.

But as his analyst, my task consists in keeping in my mind and his that the fleshly being in front of me and the text he (and too often I) mistake him for are one and the same – which is harder than you'd think. *I is an other*, Rimbaud famously declares, reminding me of the sense in which F. might be exactly right to speak of himself as someone else, an infinitely intriguing stranger. But analysis is nothing if not a space and time in which to introduce the I to this Other, to nurture a little contact between them. Although analysis is also the place where you're liable to discover just how unbearable it is to be both the raging madman and frightened child you thought you were merely talking about.

There's a memory of early childhood, related in the first weeks of F.'s analysis, which resurfaces in my mind and his associations. 'I was four or five. My mother left me outside a department store and told me to stay where I was, she'd be back in a few minutes. Rooted to the spot, I became restless and began to pace and hop about. I jumped and landed in a dirty puddle at the very moment a lady walked by hand in hand with her little girl. The girl wore a pristine white coat which was instantly streaked and spattered with muddy water. The mother scolded me furiously, wanting to know what I was doing jumping about unaccompanied in the street like that. I remember when my mother returned feeling very sad and dirty and alone.'

Perhaps you can hear an allegory here of childhood and its ordinary trauma and despair. Your mother, who can accompany and be accompanied by you through life's vast and intricate byways, can by the same token abandon you to it and to your own self, to your nameless dread of being alone, to your overbearing aggression and excitability, to the corrosive envy with which you soil the perfection you lack, to the terrors induced and dangers provoked by your omnipotence and helplessness. 'I remember . . . feeling very sad and dirty and alone,' says F., very nearly convincing both of us he's speaking about the past.

> No one moulds us again out of earth and clay,
> no one conjures our dust.
> No one.
>
> Praised be your name, no one.
> For your sake
> we shall flower.
> Towards you.
>   Paul Celan, 'Psalm'

The negative of him is more real than the positive of you, a war-traumatized patient tells Winnicott, referring to her former analyst. In other words, she feels the absence of the analyst she's lost more keenly and immediately than the presence of the analyst she has.

You can hear the echo of her plaintive, melancholy protest,

transposed to the cosmic plane of theology, in the opening stanzas of Celan's 1963 poem. If the biblical Psalmist is a flower reaching out of the dark in certain hope of finding the infinitely nourishing and protective light of Someone, Celan's Psalmist gropes instead in the blind despair of a fall into the void of No one. Perhaps this is the state of *unthinkable anxiety* into which, according to Winnicott, the youngest infant is thrown when made to experience her own helplessness. The more she intuits the absence of a mother's form-giving psychic and bodily hold, the more she's liable to internal disintegration, experienced as a fatally vertiginous *falling for ever*.

A nothing/ we were, are, shall/ remain, flowering:/ the nothing-, the/ no one's rose, runs the next stanza. To be held by the void is to be voided, drained of substance, a nothing-flower (*Die Niemandsrose* is the volume in which 'Psalm' appears) raised and cultivated by *no one*. And yet this *no one's rose* flowers nonetheless, like an infant consigned to seek and find only *no one*, to an eternal reiteration of her own helplessness.

The function of religion, writes Freud in his most polemical treatment of the subject, *The Future of an Illusion*, is to arm human beings with *a store of ideas . . . built up from the material and memories of the helplessness of . . . childhood*, against the terrifying anonymity and indifference of the universe, and so *to make his helplessness tolerable*.

Freud anticipates here the New Atheist assault on religion as infantile consolation, a clinging to magical thinking in defiance of the intolerably harsh truths of the external (or grown-up) world. And yet there's an important difference between Dawkins's 'delusional' and Freud's 'illusory' religion. A delusion is a wholesale and systematic distortion, a screen of untruth blocking the mind's capacity to perceive reality. An illusion, on the other hand, is an essential element in apprehending reality.

Religious illusion, Freud is suggesting, is psychically if not externally real, an organic outgrowth of the experience of childhood helplessness, rather than an elaborate contrivance aimed at shielding you from it. His allegiance to the positivistic ideal of science means that the renunciation of this illusion can be seen by him only as a necessary moment in the intellectual evolution of humanity. And yet if religion replicates in cultural form the functions of maternal containment (as well as paternal discipline), the experience of religious disillusion will as likely arouse in us the disorganized terror of the child as the self-possession of the adult. And is there a more compelling attestation to Winnicott's insight into the secret, collusive intimacy between omnipotence and helplessness than the great texts of religious tradition? Augustine assures us that the best chance of deep mutual understanding between people is to stand together in the light of God. Yet the corollary of this observation is that, left to the shadows of profane life, you're doomed to incarceration in the desperate, uncomprehending privacy of the self. The biblical Psalmist, calls *min hametzar, de profundis, out of the depths*, with the loved child's untroubled faith in finding the infinitely protective Hand of Someone: *The LORD is for me among those who help me*, declares Psalm 118. But isn't this anticipation of divine help tacitly conditioned and forever haunted by the spectre of helplessness, by the abyssal terror of reaching out and finding only nothingness, of *flowering towards no one*?

Apparently opposed to one another, the biblical Psalmist and Celan are in fact precariously close. The positive religious scenario of the creature under the protection of a loving God has a clandestine companion in its own negative, the Protector turned Abandoner, Torturer, Destroyer. Even His son meets his abjectly bloody end wondering why his Father has forsaken him. In the absence of the reassuring Someone of tradition, there is only *No one*, a gossamer-thin presence, to separate Celan's Psalmist from the formless terror of the *state anterior to language*, from the void of absolute helplessness. The New Atheist reduction of the God of the three monotheisms to the Father who preserves his believers from worldly harm, who offers reassuringly facile answers to painfully difficult questions, takes no account of this more troubling and enigmatic God. Religious tradition is host not only to the God who bathes us in His benign light, but also to the God of Celan's Psalmist, the No one who leaves us in darkness.

The God of the Hebrew Bible who has loomed so large in my own imaginative life has never felt very consolatory or enlightening. He is demanding, capricious, as menacing in His enigmatic distance as in His blinding immediacy, speaking a language that touches that of His creatures only at the edges. At the climax of his relentless ordeal, Job, chastened and exhausted by God's hectoring encomium to His absolute power, renounces the presumptuousness of his earlier protests: *Therefore have I uttered that which I understood not, Things too wonderful for me, which I knew not.* God's use of His creatures' language to talk to them fosters the illusion of His intelligibility. Only suffering, inexplicable and irredeemable, can shatter Job's faith in this illusion, and bring him up against the truth of his helpless incomprehension.

The pietistic injunction, common to all confessions, to walk in the ways of God, misses Job's point: divine and human logic are radically incommensurable, no one can know these ways and remain human. Abraham's godly readiness to sacrifice Isaac, Kierkegaard suggests in *Fear and Trembling*, requires a total suspension of human ethics, a willingness to become a murderer in the name of unquestioning solidarity with the divine. The place of God, or the primal father, is a lonely one. I can do whatever I desire, God effectively tells Job and his companions, indeed there's no meaningful difference between what I desire and what I do, no gap between My wish and its fulfilment, which also means that you can never hope to understand Me, and I can never hope to be understood, and My use of recognizably human words to tell you this shouldn't lull you into imagining we speak the same language. In God's absolute power, you see reflected your own helplessness and incomprehension.

In the famous final chapter of his 1913 book *Totem and Taboo*, a psychoanalytic anthropology of the origins of religion, Freud suggests that human communities are forged out of their collective renunciation of divine omnipotence, the wish to occupy the place of God. Or in the case of so-called tribal culture, they renounce the place of the *violent and jealous father who keeps all the females for himself and drives away his sons as they grow up*. In Freud's rather generalized and much criticized 'history' of the tribal psyche, the excluded brothers, bound together in fear and resentment, one day *came together, killed and devoured their father and so made an end of the patriarchal horde*. In murdering their envied sovereign, they experienced an awed remorse at the magnitude of their deed, a remorse that united them in a mutually enforced imperative: no one can seek to take the dead father's place. Your private desires must be subordinated to the collective good; you must submit, not to the unintelligible violence of the tyrant within, but to the shared understanding of the fraternity without.

This impossible dilemma of fraternity, internalized by you, me and every other neurotic, is captured in Freud's observation, at once banal and dazzling, that *sexual satisfaction is essentially the private affair of each individual*. A neurosis is an irresolvable struggle over how much to surrender to, and how much to renounce, this private quest for satisfaction. Should you identify with the

voracious Father who *keeps all the females for himself* or with
the abstemious brothers who preserve themselves from such
dangerous pleasures? The spoils of gratified desire – the limitless
sex and riches and power – may be unbearably alluring. But
they come with the one, lethal drawback of being a *private affair*.
Because it belongs to no one but you, your desire makes you
a tyrant to yourself and a stranger to all others. Freud, banal
and dazzling once again, observes that *sexual desires do not unite
men but divide them*. To pursue your own sexual desires is to risk
provoking the envious enmity of your fellow human beings, to
set yourself apart from the shared interest of the fraternity.

This is why Meg Ryan's faked orgasm in *When Harry Met
Sally* never fails to make me laugh – for that glorious moment,
the shared language of the deli, manifest in the reassuring hum
of commerce and friendship, is silenced by the singular language
of gasps and groans and stray words, signifying nothing. The
crowd stare in mute bewilderment, as though confronted, just
here amid the busy pleasures of shared food and conversation,
where human beings seem most reassuringly intelligible to one
another, with their essential unintelligibility. Your 'sex face' is
an object of frequent hilarity only because it would otherwise
be a source of terror, an image of retreat into the impenetrably
private cell of your self, where no one can reach you.

Chapter 11 of Genesis famously asks us to imagine a time
when *the whole earth was of one language and one speech*. The
bloodless skirmish that ensues between the people of earth and
the God of heaven is a striking inversion of Freud's story of the
murder of the primal father. Like the terrorized fraternity, the
people resolve to unite and break God's monopoly on celestial
power: *Come, let us build us a city, and a tower, with its top in heaven*.
The medieval Rabbinic commentator Rashi is unambiguous as
to the people's murderous underlying aim: *to wage war against*

God, as he puts it, to effect nothing less than a cosmic regime change.

The project immediately alerts God to the dangers of his creatures' linguistic unity. *Behold*, Genesis has Him say to Himself, *they are one people and they have all one language and this is what they begin to do and now there will not be withheld from them anything which they purpose to do. One people* and *one language*: each member of the multitude taking their assigned place in a single, integral body, working in seamless concert to a common purpose. What God perceives, in other words, is a human race undivided by the friction of competing private desires, rendered fully transparent to one another by the shared power of words. So that the divine resolution to *confound there their language, that they may not understand one another's speech* can be heard not only as the creation of many languages and speech communities, but as the insinuation of duplicity, ambiguity and suspicion into all speech, into human consciousness itself.

Curiously, rather than perform his counter-revolutionary alchemy from above, God descends into the city: *Come*, He exhorts Himself, *let us go down, and confound there their language*, less now the supernal destroyer menacing his people from above than a wily undercover saboteur concealed among them. Unlike the primal father, hamstrung by his faith in his own brute strength and so vulnerable to the force of sheer numbers, God pre-empts the attempted celestial coup, waging psychological warfare below before the people can ascend to military warfare above.

The bodily helplessness of the generation of the Flood, victims first to the rapacity of their insatiable carnality and then to the merciless judgement of God, is now compounded by the psychic helplessness of the generation of Babel. The unsuspecting mutual trust that makes them such a credible threat to divine rule becomes their maximal point of vulnerability – belief in the indestructible unity of their one language leaves them powerless against the strangeness of another. *Confounded* and *scattered*, the people of earth are brought up against their terrifying opacity to one another and so, perhaps, to themselves as well. For isn't the moment the other speaks a different language, breaking the ties of mutual intelligibility, the point at which you lose your intelligibility to yourself, the point at which you can no longer be sure you speak even your own language? Haven't you become, alongside yourself, *someone else*? God's ambiguous gift to humanity, the Babel story suggests, is privacy, the blessing and curse of being forever obscure and fatally interesting to one another.

Friday 13th Part XII, A Nightmare on Elm Street 8: Freddy vs. Jason, Saw 8: 3D, Halloween 8: Resurrection, Puppet Master X: Axis Rising, Child's Play 6: Curse of Chucky. Why is it that the horror genre, and especially the schlock-horror genre, as though mimicking its monstrously death-proof creations, is such a fecund generator of sequels? The commercial imperative can't on its own account for how and why it is that the genre lends itself so well to its own unending iteration.

Horror movies can't stop replaying the same basic scenario – roughly formulated, something unimaginably terrible, emanating from somewhere beyond the reach of the known world that might be called evil or madness or dream-life or death or history, is threatening to hurt and kill you. The horror movie, in other words, is a recreation of the original condition of human helplessness, of the infantile fantasy, painstakingly reconstructed by Melanie Klein, of the world as a terrorizing barrage of *bad objects*.

Sequels, after all, aren't a phenomenon confined to the cinema. Freud, you might say, saw the sequel, and especially the compulsively proliferating sequel, as a or even the most basic predicament of human experience. Something in you, as he sees it, prefers to *repeat* than to *remember* – remembering here meaning not only, as in the popular caricature of psychoanalysis, to recall to yourself an ordinarily or grossly traumatic past, but to come into awareness of the things you've done and continue to do, in your mind, in the world, with yourself, with others, all in spite of your unconscious knowledge that you'll only end up the victim.

You're your own worst enemy. Poets from Sophocles to Radiohead are forever reminding us that the saltiest spot in any wound is the knowledge that you and only you inflicted it. In tidily condensing the insight, the daily commonplace or tragic chorus or rock lyric provides the misleading assurance that you possess it. The fact that everyone knows that you're both author and victim of your suffering, that it's a familiar nugget of psychological folk wisdom, ensures that it escapes possession as anything more than a dead phrase, a verbal talisman against the pain of really *remembering*, of listening to rather than blindly repeating the words.

Even after many years of reading psychoanalysis, of lying and sitting on one or other side of the couch, I'm not sure I can believe that I'm complicit in my own suffering, that I'd rather do what I'd much rather not do than see what it is I'm doing. There are patches of analysis during which your life can start to resemble precisely one of those horror franchises comprised of interminable and increasingly preposterous sequels, storylines that pretend to be new while brazenly trotting out the same tired, grisly scenario, condemning you to watch yourself blunder into the very place the marauding serial killer or zombie or demon is lying reliably in wait. There's no psychoanalysis worth the name that doesn't include periods of wishing you'd never heard of stupid fucking psychoanalysis, never had the idea of talking aimlessly to this infuriatingly impassive ear and quietly ironizing mouth that won't let you get away with just muddling along in the harmlessly wretched way you know best, stumbling haplessly into your preferred disasters.

What is this compulsion to re-enact the scene of your original helplessness? Freud provides an answer to this question in perhaps his most celebrated piece of behavioural observation. In *Beyond the Pleasure Principle*, he describes his toddler grandson throwing a bobbin over the edge of his cot and emitting *a loud, long-drawn-out 'o-o-o-o'*, deciphered by Freud as the German *fort*, gone. He then reels it back in *with a joyful 'da' [there]*.

This apparently innocuous scene raises two disturbing questions. First, what does this insistently repeated drama represent? The disappearance and return of the bobbin, says Freud, plays out the quotidian trauma of his mother's absences, with their implicit but harrowing message that he can drop out of her physical and psychic view, that she has things and people on her mind other than him. Second, and more importantly, if this scene is so painful, why does the little boy keep replaying it? Why, in Freud's seminal phrase, *the compulsion to repeat*? Perhaps, he suggests, because repetition is endowed in the infant's mind (and later in the infantile mind of the adult) with the magical capacity to transform the original trauma. Where in the first instance of maternal absence, the boy experiences himself as insuperably helpless, he becomes, through its playful re-enactments, the triumphant author and master of the scene: *by repeating it*, says Freud, *unpleasant though it was, he took on an **active** part*.

You repeat the experience of helplessness in the impossible hope of vanquishing it, of finally preventing Jason or Freddy Krueger or Chucky or Jigsaw from torturing and murdering you yet again. The horror film is a cultural monument to helplessness and your inability to bear it.

There may be a hint here as to why one of the greatest, as well as the most sadistically unwatchable, contributions to the horror genre is also a kind of annulment of it, a grenade tossed casually into its heart, blasting apart the very possibility of the sequel.

About three years ago, I told my film buff friend K. I'd sat down the previous evening to watch Michael Haneke's 2007 *Funny Games* (a shot-for-shot US remake of his 1997 German-language original). I was grimly aware of its premise – two young men enter a prosperous family home and proceed gleefully to torture the parents and child over the course of a night, culminating in the murder of all three. I'd also known that Haneke intended the film as a severe polemic against the mainstream media's packaging of violence as a consumable pleasure that simultaneously arouses and numbs your voyeuristic sadism.

In the event this made no odds. Perhaps I was just getting too old, but after twenty minutes I'd found myself unable to watch any longer and switched off.

'Well, that's good,' K. said on hearing this, 'you actually understood it.'

Somehow his remark enabled me to return to the film and see it out to the bitter end. Only if you can't watch it, K. was hinting, only if it entirely short-circuits the possibility of your enjoying it, can you say you've understood it. With each gratuitous outrage, each new psychic and physical violation, each new step in the victims' terrorized humiliation, I sank a little deeper into the abyssal mirror of my own impotence. In *Funny Games*, there are notorious moments of knowingly manipulated excitement: the young son escapes to the neighbouring house, turns a rifle on his pursuer and fires it, only to find the barrel empty; the wife grabs a shotgun and shoots dead one of the torturers, only to have the other pick up a remote control and rewind the sequence we've just seen, reversing his partner's killing and snatching the shotgun before she can reach it.

At this and other moments, the more assured of the psycho-pathic couple turns directly to you and interrogates your motives for watching. Haven't you had enough? Do you imagine you'll be rewarded with some gratifying generic cliché, a turning of tables, an audacious flight, a triumph over evil? And so all your stupid narrative pleasures, all the anticipated gratifications you've internalized in the course of your cultural (and not just your cultural) life now confront you on screen.

What is it this mirror's showing you? Who is it you become at these moments of excitable hope, as you will the boy to shoot, or grab for the shotgun with his mother? Haven't you become Freud's grandson, the infant compulsively replaying the scene of his own helplessness? Like the toddler, you fantasize a triumphal inversion, feel for just a moment the predatory bloodlust of the victim turned predator, the helpless turned omnipotent. It's out of this fantastical victory over your own helplessness that sequels are born.

There can be no sequel to *Funny Games*, which is why it's at once a contribution to and cancellation of the horror genre. It plays out the drama of helplessness while depriving you of the compensatory fantasy of its reversal, killing off the logic of the sequel.

By the time the film had ended, with its malevolently con-spiratorial wink towards the resumption of the murderous cycle, I felt as though the entire network of muscles holding up the expressive life of my face was on the verge of collapse. How could the logic of its narrative – that if psychopathic killers hold you captive you're going to end up dead – be so obvious and yet so traumatically shocking? Perhaps because, in the face of my passion not to know, obviousness has startlingly little effect.

The following morning, I felt a curious and inexplicable calm on recalling the film, as though the pincer hold of helplessness on my nervous system was a little looser, as though having crashed and burned its way through my defences, the film could now leave me in peace, freed from the anxious need for sequels, freed from hate and fear of, to recall Levi one last time, *the dark and truncated language of a person who is about to die and is alone.*

8

The Disgrace of Being Human

A few minutes into the first session of the first morning of the very first day in my new consulting room. In the nervy grip of so many beginnings, my listening already felt a bit guarded, as though defending against some imminent catastrophe. Peering into the window behind me, I noted uneasily the gaps yawning between the slats of the blind: at just past seven a.m. on a late summer day, we were visible to anyone who cared to peer in. And with this very observation, I saw two uniformed police officers stride purposefully down to this basement, one of them catching my eye with a glance that felt as accusatory as his gratuitously prolonged buzz of the intercom.

Fearful, like some low-rent Joseph K., of being *suddenly arrested*, I apologized to the patient, cut off in mid-flow, and left the room to answer the door and the impending charge, unspecified but undoubtedly grave.

The door opened to the officer's pinched stare, partially masking the colleague standing so claustrophobically close behind him that for an infinitesimal moment I was convinced he was going to hiss under his breath, for godsake, man, help me shake this bloody clown, he will not leave me alone!, before he actually did say, 'Is there a problem sir?'

For some reason I took him to be asking me about the session he had just interrupted, which after all was confidential. In any case, he didn't wait for an answer, but briskly elaborated: 'We've had a complaint, sir. A loud disturbance here? Is there a problem?'

In some barely accessible corner of my mind, a dim light shed itself on the logic of the police state.

'Not here. I work here.' As I said this, I realized I wasn't sure what relevance it had.

'Do you mind if I check for myself, sir?', a question whose strictly rhetorical status he quickly confirmed by gliding the few steps past me to the door of my consulting room, his idiot companion shuffling behind and, again without awaiting a response, opened it. A frozen moment as he registered the young man now sat at the edge of my couch, a six-foot-two rabbit in the headlights of a speeding police car. I was trying hard to recover my thinking self, but the one word that seemed to survive the treacherous passage from my mind to my inner ear was, unhelpfully, Jesus.

'Everything all right, sir?' he asked in newly softened tones, as though to reassure him he need not be scared of me any more.

'Mmm, yeah. Fine,' the young man replied.

Perhaps it was the dim stillness that saved me from further questioning, the eerily undisturbed state of a room in which, from the perspective of a police officer, absolutely nothing happens. All I know is that, muttering words I have entirely forgotten, he and his shadow disappeared with the same casualness with which they appeared, leaving the two of us to our traumatized bemusement.

Hindsight smugly reproaches me. I should have done better in protecting the integrity of the room, in preventing the Kafka-driven fantasies aroused by the apparition of the Law's representatives from breaching the internal and external boundaries of my analytic space.

It's in this same consulting room that I sit now. Where else to begin the end of this book than in this crucible of private life? Here at this desk, where I've sat in the short and long intervals between sessions tapping the keys of an undersized Toshiba, calling up the ghosts of memory to usher in each chapter. I spend a lot of time scanning the white walls and paintwork cracks of this room, the shadow play of the standard lamp, all bathed in the streaks of grey glare coming through the narrow apertures of the venetian blind.

Psychoanalysts spend a good deal of time talking among themselves about the spoken and unspoken dramas staged inside these walls, teasing out the spectral events unfolding in the theatre of psychic reality. As those police officers demonstrated, there can be no drama without a stage or screen on which it can unfold uninterruptedly. This simple observation was the basis for a new focus in analytic theory and practice from the 1950s on the setting or frame of the clinical process. Psychoanalysis, suggested the Argentinian analyst José Bleger in 1967, involves not only *a process that is studied, analysed, and interpreted; but it also includes a frame, that is to say, a 'non-process', in the sense that it is made up of constants within whose bounds the process takes place.* These constants include a room kept free of intrusions, reliably timed sessions at regular intervals, charged at a fee changeable only by agreement – without all of which the stability of the process is precarious at best.

When you look at the walls you're noticing the unquestioned yet vital condition of any creative process. Four decades before Bleger, Virginia Woolf insisted that the process of writing was similarly dependent on this *non-process*, the background constants of adequate space, time and money, the agglomeration of which she famously named *a room of one's own*. Women were marginalized from literature, she implied, because deprived of the universal and necessary conditions for the life of writing to begin at all. Psychoanalysis and writing share the same, irreducible need for this external and internal room.

I cannot describe the 'dumbness' of the frame but only the moment when it reveals itself, when it has stopped being dumb, writes Bleger. The walls are imperceptible until they're forced into sight by someone or something. Before it's anything else, before it's an outpouring of emotion, a narrative of distress, a retreat into silence, an analytic session is a guaranteed spatial and temporal *room of one's own*, its walls sufficiently impregnable that you never have to notice them. Perhaps this is what I should have told the officer.

So here, in this room of my own, I've sat staring at the walls, an extension of, but also a relief from, the blank glare of the computer screen, a different and less persecuting surface of inscription. I stare until they're overlain by a story and the wish to tell it. Mind, room, paper, analyst – different addressees to whom to tell what you have to say.

A frame is called for as soon as the self begins the struggle to make itself heard. Think of the role a mother plays for her young infant. He clambers over her in ruthlessly loving indifference, grabbing her hair to hoist himself up, dribbling over the front of her dress, clawing her face, at once intrusively aware of and rudely oblivious to her status as a separate person. What Bleger calls the *dumbness* of the frame is something like this unquestioned givenness, the knowledge that the mother (or the analyst, or the room) in spite of her quiet discretion is, in the British psychoanalyst Enid Balint's words, *absolutely there*. What's at stake here is the child's or patient's unthought knowledge that there's someone who can bear to witness and contain his suffering, excitement and confusion, whose thereness isn't conditional but absolute and unquestionable. It's the quality Emmy von N. looked for and, not without her own creative efforts, eventually found in Freud. She wanted not the perceptive illumination of her anxieties and fantasies, but a human ear to receive the formless, unpredictable flow of whatever she had to say, to enable her to become *the patient*, as Balint puts it, *occupied in finding his own words or actions*.

But in analysis as in parenting, it can't always be this way. There will be times when this thereness is called into question, when the frame is pulled out of the leaden dumbness and obscurity of the dark. The mother screams reflexively at the guileless violence of her infant, or only slightly less reflexively at the adolescent who treats this place like a hotel, implicitly demanding that they see her rather than simply take her for granted. Or the analyst retaliates unconsciously against the patient's provokingly persistent lateness by ending the session early, or late, letting her know he has his feelings too. Being *absolutely there*, letting the child or patient tell what she has to say without intruding your own wish, demand or claim, is perhaps as hard as parenting or analysis gets. What makes a good hotel? A place whose ministrations and gratifications are both constant and discrete, a kind of fantastical mother whose unstinting care demands no gratitude, no awareness even. Whereas a bad hotel is one that forces you to see the resentment aroused by the strain of taking care of you. A bad hotel is a frame that won't stay dumb – which may be why *Fawlty Towers* is so unfailingly funny. But no parent or analyst is, or indeed should be, so good as to remain dumb in all circumstances.

Every region of experience requires a frame. In most cases, it disappears imperceptibly into the process it frames. The cinema screen and the film are indistinguishable for as long as the projector's working. The frame's significance comes into focus only at the point its presence is felt, *when it has stopped being dumb*.

One way that the unconscious distinguishes itself from conscious life is in the seeming absence of a regulating frame. *There is no such thing as an unconscious no*, Freud wrote more than once, meaning that the principle of negation, of a limit on your desires and wishes, the sovereign law of conscious life, goes unrecognized in the unconscious. This may be why the psychoanalytic literature on dreams, Freud's famous *royal road to the unconscious*, so rarely seems to note the presence of a frame.

A not altogether inaccurate version of psychoanalysis conceives the dream as a piece of anarchic psychic freeplay, gleefully spilling over the frames of time, space, logic and desire, defying all the strictures of waking reality. This conception was put in question by a series of articles written in the late 1940s and early 1950s by the American analyst Bertram Lewin. The first of these begins with his observation of the presence within the dream of a *screen – the surface on to which a dream appears to be projected . . . present in the dream though not necessarily seen*. Lewin is alerted to the screen by a young female patient who, just as she's about to relate a dream, tells him '*it turned over away from me, rolled up, and rolled away from me – over and over like two tumblers*'.

The patient's dream, in other words, withdraws itself, rolls itself up, at the very moment of display: *the dream screen with the dream on it bent over backwards away from her, and then like a carpet or canvas rolled up and off into the distance*. But what is this screen, asks Lewin, and why should it make itself felt in this way? He finds the answer in the earliest experiences of falling asleep. The newborn infant's sleep begins in the meeting of his cheek with a flattening surface, most likely the pillowy flesh of his mother's breast, a meeting that becomes the prototype for sleep in his life to come. The state of sleep is brought about, in other words, by a fall into a zero-state of psychic activity. *The blank dream screen,* writes Lewin, *is the copy of primary infantile sleep*. Dreams are an insinuation of wakefulness into this nirvana, an internal saboteur of sleep's psychic nullity.

This is a very instructive refinement of Freud's description of dreams as *guardians of sleep*. Dreams, says Freud, ensure the dreamer remains in the state of sleep that body and psyche demand. But, following Lewin, it may be more precise to assign this function of guardianship to the dream *screen*. The wakeful psychic activity of the dream content is possible only because the blank dream screen, the representative of the wish to sleep, provides a surface on which it can write or paint or speak itself.

So what happened when the young woman's dream *rolled away* as she was about to relate it to her analyst? You'll recognize the predicament from your own experience of sitting groggily at the edge of your bed, clamping shut your eyelids in the desperate and vain attempt to keep hold of your unstoppably fugitive dream. *The day*, writes Walter Benjamin in his essay on Proust, *unravels what the night has woven*. The dream, it seems, refuses to be captured in the light of day. It insists on returning to its rightful nocturnal home, on reclaiming its essential privacy. The rolling away of the dream screen proclaims the dream as belonging to the dreamer. It asserts the right of the dream, and all the wishes and anxieties it expresses, to remain within the bounds of the dreamer's sleep. In locating itself so defiantly in the inviolable interior, the dream affirms its singular origin in the unconscious of this person and no other. The dream isn't, in this respect at least, as a lazy commonplace would suggest, like a movie, isn't like a product in the cultural domain that anyone can watch and make their own.

If you can't suppress a yawn when someone starts to tell you last night's dream, this is why – the verbal and visual language in which the dream speaks, even when it seems perfectly recognizable, is essentially meaningless when wrenched from the frame of sleep, from the living texture of the dreamer's unconscious. You can interpret dreams in analysis only because analysis provides the frame, the blank screen on which the dream can start to signify its own, irreducibly private meaning. Dreams are compelling in an analytic session for precisely the reason they're unspeakably tedious at parties. Analysis, the private space in which the patient can be *alone (that is to say, in the presence of someone)*, recreates the conditions in which a dream can become meaningful once more.

What, then, of the team of Berkeley neuroscientists seeking to capture and reconstruct visual activity in the brain, opening up the possibility of *watching one's own dream on YouTube*? Here you find yourself at the cutting edge of what the cultural and scientific impresario and commentator John Brockman calls, following Marshall McLuhan, *the collective externalized mind*. The very notion of an irreducible interiority, on Brockman's view, is quaintly anachronistic. The virtual culture of the Internet transports the self beyond the *private and personal mindset* associated with the Freudian unconscious, and into a zone of pure exteriority, in which the individual mind has effectively turned itself inside out and plugged itself into *the mind we all share*.

What more total realization of a *collective externalized mind* than broadcasting the sleeping unconscious on YouTube, the utopian prospect brought into sight by the Berkeley study? Its lead author, Shinji Nishimoto, served along with two other members of his team as subjects for an experiment which saw them undergo a series of MRI scans each several hours long. The scans measured blood flow in the visual cortex while the subjects watched a sequence of movie trailers. A computer correlated visual patterns in the trailers with corresponding activity in the brain. The research team then fed *18 million seconds of random*

YouTube videos into the computer program so that it could predict the brain activity that each film clip would most likely evoke in each subject. Those clips most similar to the clips the subject had likely seen (as indicated by the scans) were then *merged to produce a blurry yet continuous reconstruction of the original movie.*

The massive archive of YouTube material served the same role in the recreation of the brain's visual activity as paint in the making of a painting. The recreations didn't show us the mind in its naked immediacy, didn't turn it inside out and display its actual contents. What's being promised isn't the projection of the dream as it is dreamt, but a reconstructive representation using as its medium the accumulated debris of our culture, as though 18 million seconds of YouTube can be assumed to encompass everything a modern mind could contain.

The use of a scan of neural activity to reconstruct internal visual experience is unarguably a remarkable technological achievement. But when the talk is of, say, *watching one's own dream on YouTube*, the fact of technological achievement is being fatally conflated with its meaning.

Assume that this nascent technology could eventually reconstruct the content of a dream, setting aside the immediate snag that there'd be no means of judging the accuracy of the reconstruction given that the dreamer sleeps through her dream and so can tell you only if it resembles her memory of it rather than the dream itself, which are two very different things.

Even allowing that you could see on YouTube exactly what you'd seen in your dream, the two experiences would still have very little to do with one another. Seeing your dream during waking life is a world away from dreaming your dream during sleep. What is excluded by the YouTube version is the dream's origin in its own frame, the dreamer's sleeping mind. Torn off their screen, the contents of the dream become so meaninglessly interchangeable they could be random bits of YouTube video. In the Berkeley scenario, dreams have effectively been (Blanchot again) *separated from themselves and destroyed in order to be known, subjugated, communicated*. The dream is a dream precisely because it is created by and accessible to the dreamer alone. In separating the dream from the private life of the dreamer, you destroy it. The dream is communicated at the price of its meaning.

Brockman's ideal of a world without interiority misses an obvious difficulty. Freud, remember, found in the fact of words the record of a troubled passage from the inside to the outside of the mind, a passage in which *something*, the very interior thing itself, is always lost. The dream you experience in your sleep, forged out of the singular contents of your mind, exists only in and for you. The dream you might one day see on YouTube, forged out of the stuff of the external world, will exist for everyone. The dream screen is what distinguishes the two. It is the dream's essential reticence, its impulse to roll itself up before it is revealed to another, or to the entire world.

Is it possible that the private life has become so entirely devalued, the world so thoroughly reduced to its external expressions, that these two dreams could be considered the same, or only trivially different?

If the screen ensures the dream's privacy and secures its proper place in your sleeping mind, why seek to eliminate it? Perhaps the question whispers its own answer. Perhaps the fantasy of *watching one's own dream on YouTube* is of driving a wedge between dreams and sleep, of dissolving their supposedly indissoluble partnership. Freud suggests a powerful motive for this fantasy with the third and most lethal of his famous triad of blows in the history of human knowledge – that most of your psychic life goes on without you knowing anything about it, that you're not even master in your own house. Where is this humiliating truth visited on you more persistently than in your sleep?

Your dreams trouble or amuse or excite or frighten or puzzle you, not just on account of their specific content, but equally because they happen in your absence, reminding you of the strangers wreaking havoc in your house when you're not home. Waking life offers all kinds of stratagems for denying or trivializing unconscious experience. If you think hard enough, you can always find a perfectly reasonable explanation for why you forgot your husband's birthday or called your wife by your sister's name. But your dreams are pieces of unconscious life you can't so readily explain away. Dreams make a fool of you, thinking and feeling for you behind your sleeping back, a perpetual yet unacknowledged outrage of everyday life. What more perfect vengeance on millennia of psychic dispossession than to snatch dreams from their hiding place in sleep, to humiliate them the way they've humiliated you and everyone else down the ages. Ha! There you are on YouTube – not so clever now, are you?

Perhaps this revenge fantasy can cast a bit of light on the growing phenomenon of lifelogging, the practice of recording and broadcasting your life minute by minute, using wearable cameras that stream video live to the Internet, installing webcams in all private spaces, storing all phone and email communications and even, in its most radical form, installing nano-sensors in the body to record vital functions. The ambiguous promise of such a project is a spectral double of your lived life, digitally archived and searchable.

You don't have to think long about the lifelog before it triggers an avalanche of ethical and political anxieties regarding the privacy of those who enter it, wittingly or not, its effect on the logger's personal and professional relationships, its vulnerability to subpoena by law enforcement agencies and corporate exploitation. All these anxieties have their source in the same tendency – the wrenching of life from its frame, from its original location in a singular private self. As soon as life escapes the bounds of its own mind and body, uncomfortable questions arise over where it belongs, on whom and what it can intrude.

The question also arises, as with the YouTube dream, of the precise relationship between the original life and its digital double. Searching through the copious blog entries on the lifelog phenomenon reveals an overriding tone of utopian enthusiasm. Personal and social problems, from festering arguments to violent crime, could be resolved by appeal to the log. The progress of a lifelong love, a child's growth, a fatal illness can all be relived, reorganized, reinterpreted.

The sci-fi delirium passes over a basic snag: the external record of life can't be equated with its experience, any more than your dream can be equated with its broadcast. Take the case of a quarrel, say a painful and terrible fall-out with a lifelong friend. Your log of the showdown may indeed clarify exactly who said what and when. But this assumes that this is what you want to know, that this is what needs knowing. Torn from its origin in the live feelings of two loving and hating souls, the exchange becomes an external spectacle rather than an emotional confrontation. The presence of the camera will distort the argument, intruding the wily calculations of posterity into the immediate fog of rage and hurt. You can no more authentically make war than make love under the gaze of a camera.

But even if you bracket off the distorting effect of the camera, it remains doubtful whether the meaning and so the resolution of an argument can be decided by appeal to its transcript. Your insides may have engorged in righteousness as you informed your friend how sickened you were by his Olympian smugness, arrogance and self-absorption, your ear quivered in outrage as he charged you with poisonous envy of the success and admiration he so effortlessly draws to himself. The filmed record won't tell you who you were for one another in that quarrel, what it was in your inner histories and fantasies that drove you to such escalations of mutual cruelty and hate. Watched in its aftermath, the video may provide you with some masochistically gratifying drama, but at the expense of any contact with the argument as a piece of private experience, an expression of the self you don't and can't possess. The lifelog is bound to nurture a confusion of psychic with external reality.

Perhaps this confusion is the very aim, albeit unconscious, of the lifelog: to rid the self of the burden of psychic reality, to eliminate the difference between seeing and experiencing, outside and inside, to reduce life to the pictures you can take of it? Could the real aim of the lifelogger's wholesale renunciation of privacy be a divorce from his own unconscious?

Much more is at stake here than broadcasting dreams or lifelogging. The war on privacy being waged today on so many fronts begs the question as to whether the fantasy fuelling an entire culture isn't a divorce from its own unconscious, a disowning of the self's own strangeness. Behaviourism has taken over our culture's picture of human subjectivity, our ideas of how to live individually and collectively.

Positive psychology, which directs clinical treatments and academic research towards the cultivation of forms of thinking and doing that lead to happiness, and the correction of those that don't, has become increasingly influential at the level of social as well as health policy. In positive psychology and its closely allied clinical practice, cognitive behavioural therapy (CBT), the first and essential malady of the soul is erroneous or *maladaptive* thinking. CBT corrects, that is, kinks and failures in your full adaptation to reality.

To amplify and enrich the patient's sense of reality is by no means a contemptible aim for any therapist. But is reality a set of fixed verities to be pointed to, as on a Google map for the lost soul? Can the distinction between reality and our perception of it be so reassuringly lacking in ambiguity? You'd think so to listen to reputed biological psychiatrist and leading advocate of CBT Lewis Wolpert elaborate this distinction in the course of a comically vituperative attack on psychoanalysis. Speaking against the clinical efficacy of psychoanalysis at a debate at the Maudsley psychiatric hospital in March 2012, Wolpert conjured a typical scenario in cognitive therapy in order to demonstrate its superiority. *Nobody loves me*, a depressive patient complains, to which the therapist responds, *Nobody loves you?* The patient pauses before conceding, *Well, maybe my dog. I know it sounds trivial*, Wolpert glosses, *but when you show someone who's in a severe depression that there's something false in their negativity, it's a really positive step.*

The picture of psychic life implied by this vignette, the kind of entity it imagines the human soul, and indeed external reality, to be is fully consistent with the CBT framework as formulated by Aaron Beck in the late 1970s. For Beck, mental suffering is rooted in a series of cognitive biases – 'over-generalizing' or 'magnifying' the negative, 'minimizing' the positive. If you think no one loves you, that you're hideously ugly or doomed to fail in all you do, you're just not seeing straight. Notice your dog clambering over you excitedly as you walk through the door, the flirty compliment you received at the bar, the promotion you just won.

In other words, your psychic reality is a mistake, a piece of maladaptive thinking you can be cured of by seeing the difference between how things really are and how you perceive them, by purifying your gaze of its distortive, magnifying, minimizing lenses. On one side of a line is the private world in which your anxieties and fantasies grind out their fatal and persistent errors, on the other the shared world in which reality can be seen for what it is. Leave your private life behind and see what everyone else sees. Don't relate to it as a source of insight, especially not if what it sees is cruel or hateful or painful. Do not, as cognitive practitioners like to say, brood. And don't indulge the speculation, beloved of airy poets and philosophers and unscientific psychoanalysts, that the relationship between the mind and the world is a problem, a question rather than a given.

Wolpert's vignette was preceded by a furious broadside against psychoanalysis. The very notion of the unconscious, he told his audience, is *nonsense. It's monstrous, I don't know how you can take psychoanalysis seriously, it seems to me totally impenetrable.* Two dream thoughts in sequence, Freud said, are always intimately related, and I'm tempted to ask if this isn't sometimes true also of waking thoughts. Listened to on the podcast, the gentle nudging of Wolpert's imagined therapist towards right perception – *Nobody loves you?* – sounds oddly dissonant with the preceding burst of machine-gun fire against the psychoanalytic enemy.

Might this dissonance hint at the violence quietly lurking in CBT's genial war on psychic reality? The cognitive therapist undoubtedly wants to hear you tell what you have to say, but in order to show you just how wrong it is. Your private life resides in the dark because that's where it belongs, a rubbish heap of muddled thinking you'd do best to ignore.

It's unlikely to be mere coincidence, then, that during the early 1960s, as the behavioural model of mental life and clinical treatment was coming into vogue, various psychoanalysts, especially in Britain and France, were noticing the increasingly frequent appearance in their clinics and consulting rooms of a new kind of patient whose bodies and words seemed to express a radical estrangement from their own psychic lives, who appeared *out of touch*, in Winnicott's words, *with the subjective world and with the creative approach to fact*.

In a chilling chapter of his seminal 1983 book, *Shadow of the Object*, Christopher Bollas coins the term *normotic* to describe this state of self-alienation. The term hints at both an affinity with and an inversion of the more familiar *psychotic*. Instead of the inward retreat described by Freud, *into the world of fantasy and hallucination*, the normotic's oxymoronic impulse is an outward retreat into an externalized, *abnormally normal* world from which all ambiguity, strangeness and pain have been expunged, a world reduced to an infinite series of desiccated facts. This is a world in which the feeling of, say, being entirely unloved will be granted no emotional or existential significance.

Bollas was preceded, as he acknowledges, by a number of French analysts in identifying this flight into external life. The group of Parisian analysts known as the Psychosomatic School described patients coming into a psychiatric (rather than a classical psychoanalytic) setting in whom a sustained and developed inner life has never taken root, dominated by what they call *pensée operatoire* or *operational thinking*. *Operational thinking*, write Pierre Marty and Michel de M'Uzan in 1963, *essentially applies to* things, *never to products of the imagination or to symbolic expressions*. A patient caught in this mode of thinking, Marty suggests in a later article of 1968, can't even experience himself as in a state of need or pain: *the psychoanalyst has to wonder what he can do for a patient who in any case is not asking for anything because he is scarcely even suffering*.

Suffering, Bion repeatedly observes, is more a capacity than an occurrence. The capacity to suffer enables you to live your experience as yours, to feel, imagine and create it from the inside.

The operational thinker and the normotic survive the psychic demands of daily living by annulling this capacity or perhaps by never having developed it in the first place. Renouncing the hard work of discovering and cultivating a private life, the normotic identifies himself with the ready-made world of common facts. Conscious life is deprived of the unconscious activity that would ordinarily inform and enrich it – *the instrumental function of waking life*, write Marty and de M'Uzan, *tends to invade the entire field*.

In normotic life, says Bollas, emotional states are subjected to *negative hallucination*, treated as though they simply aren't there – which in a way they aren't. In the absence of the internal space that receives and processes *unconscious affects, memories and perceptions*, the external world is the only reality the normotic can lay hold of.

But isn't the normotic a kind of unconscious ideal for the behaviourist? Doesn't the behaviourist ask us to treat the representations of unconscious life, and especially those that feel dangerous, excessive, incomprehensible, as though they weren't there, to replace the interior void of lovelessness with the external fact of a clambering dog?

The primary value of private life, in the face of this assault on psychic reality, is to preserve the self's essential ambiguity, to prevent its disappearance into the daylight glare of common facts. For all his identification with the spirit of science, Freud finds the deepest affinities and echoes of his thought in the pages of Shakespeare, Goethe and Dostoevsky. More specifically, he finds in them a conception of human subjectivity, for which science hitherto had lacked a vocabulary, as radically singular, in excess of any of the laws, metrics or principles science itself can posit. This singularity, the very source of creative life, is also the intolerable burden from which human beings are perpetually trying to liberate themselves.

As the unnamed narrator, drawing his *Notes from Underground* to a close, declares, *We find it a burden being human beings – human beings with our **own** real flesh and blood, we are ashamed of it, consider it a disgrace and are forever striving to become some kind of imaginary generalized human beings*.

However much you seek to generalize yourself, to render yourself reassuringly transparent to yourself and to others, you suffer the insuperable *disgrace* of being particular, of inhabiting your *own real flesh and blood*. You can only show me the self that lives above ground by withholding the self that remains underground.

Size zero. This peculiar terminological innovation by the American fashion industry in the sizing of women's clothing (the UK equivalent, size four, ascribes at least some minimal existence to the body in question) starts in this context to sound like a very explicit expression of the *disgrace* of *our own real flesh and blood*.

The sense in the public debate on this issue is of an increasing solidarity with the body's right to be what it is, to be defined and shaped by the self it embodies, rather than railroaded into *the imaginary generalized ideal* beaming out from advertising hoardings and magazine covers.

This strength of popular feeling hasn't yet vanquished the fashion industry's entrenched preference for the size-zero model. It has, however, seemed to make its leading figures more nervous of spelling out the rationale for this preference explicitly. The argument is instead whispered: the size-zero body is favoured because it doesn't disturb the garments it displays, doesn't intrude the noisy irregularities of the flesh, but instead disappears obligingly into its clothing.

Perhaps size zero is simply fashion's relationship to the body taken to its logical conclusion. The outline of bodily form through its clothing is an intimation of the self as a creature of fleshly appetites, of desires and hungers that spill over or out of the frame that tries to contain them. It might also hint at unassuageable anxieties, of material or emotional deprivation, of internal struggles and conflicts both ordinary and extreme. Bodily form is one of the innumerable ways the obscurity of private life, the singular idiom of an unconscious, gives tacit expression to itself.

Perhaps the marketing innovation of a size zero is yet another cultural expression of the drive to eliminate this obscurity, to kill the body as a piece of psychic reality, an object of subterranean love and hate, to turn it into a mute indentured servant of the external world.

None of this, of course, is meant as a joyless denunciation of the elegance and decadence and invention fashion can embody. I can't deny the sneaky pleasure of the painstakingly stylized, desexualized erotism of the *Vogue* spread, the stagy artifice and self-consciousness of the scenarios they bring to life. They offer, in a way, the opposite pleasure to pornography – not the fantastical, finally doomed promise of revealing the sexual body's privacy, but the contrasting yet entirely complementary fantasy of causing the privacy of the body to dissolve, to be absorbed into the veil it wears for the world's gaze.

And as with pornography, the furtive pleasure soon succumbs, as you turn the pages, to a deflated exhaustion, an amplified feeling of being lumbered with the cumbersome psychic and fleshly weight of your own body, of enviously lacking the fantasized weightlessness of the images in front of you. And then there's the recurrence of the same facial expression in endless subtle variants – haunted, languid, melancholic, distracted, indifferent, but always impenetrably glassy. The severe grey trouser suit squaring the slight shoulders, on which sits a geometrically combed head scowling with pantomimic hostility; the torn silk T-shirt, teasingly whispering of now-spent passion; every image speaks of a peculiar weariness of life, the vanity of its pleasures, the stoic endurance of its emptiness.

Even here you find a precise corollary to the pornographic counterpart. Porn promises to reveal fleshly desire in all its vivid, excitable immediacy, fashion to reveal the dead end of desire, the beautifully empty shell you're left with when you renounce faith in all desires. Each flaunts its own inauthenticity, offers you a tantalizing counterfeit of live feeling.

The beautiful, writes Walter Benjamin enigmatically in his essay on Goethe, *is neither the veil nor the veiled object but the object in its veil*. Fashion tempts you with the veil, porn with the object veiled. But the living self is neither of these – neither, that is, the veil you can see nor the object you can't, neither the clothes nor the body, neither the *young woman* on display nor the *fat old man* within, but the intimate play of the two.

At every moment, the life of your self is shared between the light and the dark, to the point where you don't always know which is which. Do your clothes disguise or reveal you? Is your body really undisguised when naked? *The bride*, declares Wallace Stevens in *Notes Toward a Supreme Fiction*, speaking through the medium of Ozymandias, the Egyptian statue in whom Shelley saw the embodiment of divine beauty, *Is never naked. A fictive covering/ Weaves always glistening from the heart and mind*.

Your private life is concealed imperceptibly in your public face. No one can see the naked truth of who you are, because the self *is never naked*, however many garments it sheds, however many secrets it confesses.

Thus in this one pregnant subject of CLOTHES, rightly understood, is included all that men have thought, dreamed, done, and been: the whole external Universe and what holds it is but Clothing; and the essence of all Science lies in the PHILOSOPHY OF CLOTHES.

So pronounces Professor Diogenes Teufelsdröckh (literally 'Devil's Excrement'), the fictive German Idealist philosopher and author of the equally fictive treatise *Clothes, Their Origin and Influence,* in one of the most brilliantly unclassifiable, puzzling and so chronically under-appreciated novels in the English literary canon. *Sartor Resartus,* Thomas Carlyle's only work of imaginative fiction before turning to historical writing, is composed as an introduction by a rather anxious and doubtful English editor to Teufelsdröckh's comically dense, disorganized and purple tome. In layering so many fictions upon one another, the novel performs its own central conceit, that the truth of the human being lies in the guises he assumes, the fictions in which he conceals himself.

Among the many questions Carlyle poses in the book is what it would mean, if all you think, dream, do and are is a form of clothing, to discover yourself. If your naked self is forever garbed in what Stevens's Ozymandias calls *a fictive covering,* there can be no question of arriving at some eternal and changeless core of your being.

What you might discover instead is, as literary and sartorial specialists alike would say, your *style.* And one of the most basic expressions of your style would be your language, or, in the words of Teufelsdröckh, *the Flesh-Garment, the Body, of Thought.* Here you find infinite varieties of human idiom.

Some styles are lean, writes Teufelsdröckh, *adust, wiry, the muscle itself seems osseous; some are even quite pallid, hunger-bitten and dead-looking; while other again glow in the flush of health and vigorous self-growth.* Some, on the other hand, are *sham . . . deceptively bedizening, or bolstering it* [i.e. the *Thought-Body*] *out and as such may be called its false stuffings, superfluous show-cloaks, and tawdry woollen rags.*

What is the question concealed in this inventory of styles if not how do you want to clothe yourself? How might your styles of thinking, dreaming, doing and being, the *fictive covering* you weave around yourself, express your singularity? Isn't this the infinitely generative question opened up by Freud when he chose to let Emmy *tell me what she had to say*?

And perhaps we also find, in Teufelsdröckh's variety of styles, something like Bollas's distinction between an idiom of fate and one of destiny. The fateful style might be impoverished, *hunger-bitten* and *dead-looking*, an anonymous, size-zero idiom conveying nothing of the inner life of its speaker. Or it might be *sham*, nothing but the shallow, empty ostentation of *false stuffings* and *superfluous show-cloaks*.

What these apparently opposed styles have in common is their failure to bring the veil into a living relationship with the person it is veiling, drowning her out instead in an impoverishment or excess of style.

For a style to *glow in the flush of health and vigorous self-growth*, it need not, cannot, be in compliance with a style that's already been prescribed for it. The style that is destined rather than fated will find its own signature, its own fictions in which to tell what it has to say. To discover and cultivate this private idiom is the interminable, impossible and necessary aim of psychoanalysis, of literature, of any thought, dream, act or mode of being that aspires to creativity.

You can't borrow your dreams or fantasies or any other psychic states from outside. Your idiom takes root and grows only because it's planted in the soil of your own self. You speak or write or paint or dance or joke in the hope of showing this self to others, of making it visible and audible.

But the moment you do this, suggests Blanchot, *a disconcerting ordeal begins*. The ordeal is simply this: what you say and what the other hears won't coincide. The gratification you derive from *people taking an interest* turns to an unsettling confusion when you discover that *the interest they take in it is different from the interest that made it a pure expression of [your]self, transforms it into something different, something in which [you] do not recognise the original perfection.*

The desire to express your pure, naked self, to bring it into the light of day, can only end in frustration, in the feeling that what you most wanted to show remains in the dark. Whoever's reading or listening is liable to make of your words something quite other than what you thought you meant.

And yet I cling to this desire, in the knowledge that private life, mine and everyone else's, is finally incommunicable, that the passage between my inner life and yours is hopelessly treacherous, that most of what I've tried to claw from the interior has been lost or distorted somewhere in the tunnel that separates us. You could say, rightly, that this persistence in remaining in the dark is cause for despair. But also, and equally rightly, that it's our only hope.

Bibliography

Jean Améry, *At the Mind's Limits: Contemplations by a Survivor on Auschwitz and Its Realities*, trans. S. and S. Rosenfeld (Bloomington, IN: Indiana University Press, 1998)

Yasmin Anwar, 'Scientists use brain imaging to reveal the movies in our mind', http://newscenter.berkeley.edu/2011/09/22/brain-movies

Hannah Arendt, *The Human Condition* (New York: Doubleday Anchor, 1959)

St Augustine, *Confessions*, trans. H. Chadwick (Oxford: Oxford University Press, 1998)

Piera Aulagnier, *The Violence of Interpretation: From Pictogram to Statement*, trans. A. Sheridan (Hove: Brunner-Routledge, 2001)

Jane Austen, *Emma* (London: Penguin, 1970)

Enid Balint, 'Creative Life', *Before I Was I: Psychoanalysis and the Imagination*, ed. J. Mitchell and M. Parsons (London: Free Association Books, 1993)

A. Ben Isaiah and B. Sharfman, with H. Orlinsky and M. Charner (eds.), *The Pentateuch and Rashi's Commentary*, Volume 1, Genesis (Brooklyn, NY: S. S. and R. Publishing Co., 1977)

Walter Benjamin, 'On Language As Such and the Language

of Man', *Selected Writings 1913–1926: Volume 1*, ed. M. W. Jennings and M. Bullock, trans. E. Jephcott (Cambridge, MA: Harvard University Press, 1996)

Walter Benjamin, 'Goethe's *Elective Affinities*', ibid.

Walter Benjamin, 'Moscow', *Selected Writings 1927–1934: Volume 2*, ed. M. W. Jennings and M. Bullock, trans. E. Jephcott (Cambridge, MA: Harvard University Press, 1999)

Walter Benjamin, 'The Image of Proust', trans. H. Zohn, ibid.

Wilfred Bion, *Attention and Interpretation* (London: Karnac, 2007)

Maurice Blanchot, 'Everyday Speech', *The Infinite Conversation*, trans. S. Hanson (Minneapolis, MN: University of Minnesota Press, 1993)

Maurice Blanchot, 'Humankind', ibid.

Maurice Blanchot, 'Literature and the Right to Death', *The Work of Fire*, trans. L. Davis (Stanford, CA: Stanford University Press, 1995)

Maurice Blanchot, 'Orpheus' Gaze', *The Space of Literature*, trans. A. Smock (Lincoln, NE: University of Nebraska Press, 1982)

Maurice Blanchot, *The Writing of the Disaster*, trans. A. Smock (Lincoln, NE: University of Nebraska Press, 1986)

José Bleger, 'Psycho-Analysis of the Psycho-Analytic Frame', *International Journal of Psychoanalysis*, 48 (1967)

Christopher Bollas, *Forces of Destiny* (London: Free Association Books, 1989)

Christopher Bollas, *The Shadow of the Object* (London: Free Association Books, 1987)

Thomas Carlyle, *Sartor Resartus* (Oxford: Oxford University Press, 2008)

Paul Celan, '*La poésie ne s'impose plus, il s'expose*', *Collected Prose*, trans. R. Waldrop (Manchester: Carcanet, 1998)

Paul Celan, 'Psalm', *Selected Poems*, trans. M. Hamburger (London: Penguin, 1996)

A. Cohen (ed.), *The Book of Job* (Brooklyn, NY: Soncino Press, 1948)

A. Cohen (ed.), 'The Book of Jonah', *The Twelve Prophets*, (Brooklyn, NY: Soncino Press, 1948)

Pamela Connolly, 'The Theory Behind Shrink Rap', http://www.channel4.com/programmes/shrink-rap/articles/the-theory-behind-shrink-rap

Lydia Davis, 'Story', *Break It Down* (London: Serpent's Tail, 1996)

Lydia Davis, 'What She Knew', ibid.

Paul de Man, *Allegories of Reading: Figural Language in Rousseau, Nietzsche, Rilke and Proust* (New Haven: Yale University Press, 1979)

Fyodor Dostoyevsky, *Notes from Underground* and *The Double*, trans. R. Wilks (London: Penguin, 2009)

Orlando Figes, *The Whisperers: Private Life in Stalin's Russia* (London: Penguin, 2008)

Michel Foucault, *The Will to Knowledge: The History of Sexuality*, Volume 1, trans. R. Hurley (London: Penguin, 1998)

Sigmund Freud, *Studies on Hysteria, The Standard Edition of the Complete Psychological Works of Sigmund Freud*, Volume 2, trans. and ed. J. Strachey (London: Vintage, 2001)

Sigmund Freud, *The Interpretation of Dreams, Standard Edition*, Volumes 4 and 5

Sigmund Freud, *Fragment of an Analysis of a Case of Hysteria, Standard Edition*, Volume 7

Sigmund Freud, *Three Essays on the Theory of Sexuality, Standard Edition*, Volume 7

Sigmund Freud, *Totem and Taboo, Standard Edition*, Volume 13

Sigmund Freud, 'The Unconscious', *Standard Edition*, Volume 14

Sigmund Freud, 'A Metapsychological Supplement to the Theory of Dreams', *Standard Edition*, Volume 14

Sigmund Freud, 'Fixation to Trauma – The Unconscious', Lecture

XVIII, *Introductory Lectures on Psycho-Analysis*, *Standard Edition* Volume 16

Sigmund Freud, *From the History of an Infantile Neurosis* (The 'Wolf-Man'), *Standard Edition*, Volume 17

Sigmund Freud, 'The Uncanny', *Standard Edition*, Volume 17

Sigmund Freud, *Beyond the Pleasure Principle*, *Standard Edition*, Volume 18

Sigmund Freud, *The Ego and the Id*, *Standard Edition*, Volume 19

Sigmund Freud, *Inhibitions, Symptoms and Anxiety*, *Standard Edition*, Volume 20

Sigmund Freud, *The Future of an Illusion*, *Standard Edition*, Volume 21

Nathaniel Hawthorne, 'The Minister's Black Veil', *Tales* (New York: W. W. Norton, 1987)

Nathaniel Hawthorne, *The Scarlet Letter* (London: Penguin, 1983)

Martin Heidegger, 'The Age of the World Picture', *The Question Concerning Technology and Other Essays*, trans. W. Lovitt (New York: HarperCollins, 1982)

Martin Heidegger, 'The Nature of Language', *On the Way to Language*, trans. J. Stambaugh (New York: HarperCollins, 1982)

Invisible: Art About the Unseen, 1957–2012, exhibition catalogue (London: Hayward Gallery Publishing, 2012)

Henry James, 'The Beast in the Jungle', *Tales of Henry James* (New York: W. W. Norton, 2003)

Henry James, 'The Private Life', *The Figure in the Carpet and Other Stories* (London: Penguin, 1986)

Franz Kafka, *The Trial*, trans. W. and E. Muir (London: Vintage, 1992)

Søren Kierkegaard, *Fear and Trembling: Dialectical Lyric by Johannes de Silentio*, trans. A. Hannay (London: Penguin, 1985)

Jean Laplanche, *Essays on Otherness*, trans. and ed. J. Fletcher (London: Routledge, 1999)

Jean Laplanche, *Life and Death in Psychoanalysis*, trans. J. Mehlman (Baltimore, MD: Johns Hopkins University Press, 1985)

Darian Leader, *What Is Madness?* (London: Hamish Hamilton, 2011)

Primo Levi, 'On Obscure Writing', *Other People's Trades*, trans. R. Rosenthal (New York: Summit, 1989)

Bertram Lewin, 'Sleep, the Mouth and the Dream Screen', *Psychoanalytic Quarterly*, 15 (1946)

Pierre Marty, 'Essential Depression', trans. S. Leighton, *Reading French Psychoanalysis*, ed. D. Birksted-Breen, S. Flanders and A. Gibeault (Hove: Routledge, 2010)

Pierre Marty and Michel de M'Uzan, 'Operational Thinking', ibid.

Maudsley Debate: Wake Up to the Unconscious, http://www.kcl.ac.uk/iop/news/events/2012/March/44th-Maudsley-Debates.aspx

John Milton, *Paradise Lost*, ed. A. Fowler (Harlow: Longman, 1987)

Jemima Montagu, 'Summary', Gillian Wearing, *Signs that say what you want them to say and not Signs that say what someone else wants you to say 1992–1993*, http://www.tate.org.uk/art/artworks/wearing-im-desperate-p78348/text-summary

John Naughton, 'John Brockman: The man who runs the world's smartest website', *Observer*, 8 January 2012

Patrick Ness, *The Knife of Never Letting Go* (London: Walker Books, 2008)

Friedrich Nietzsche, *The Birth of Tragedy*, trans. F. Golffing (New York: Anchor Books, 1988)

Edgar Allan Poe, 'The Man of the Crowd', *Tales of Mystery and Imagination* (Ware: Wordsworth Editions, 1993)

Jean-Bertrand Pontalis, *Windows*, trans. A. Quinney (Lincoln, NE: University of Nebraska Press, 2003)

Arthur Rimbaud, *Collected Poems*, trans. O. Bernard (London: Penguin, 1986)

Jean-Jacques Rousseau, *Confessions*, trans. A. Scholar (Oxford: Oxford University Press, 2000)

Eric Santner, *On Creaturely Life: Rilke, Benjamin, Sebald* (Chicago, IL: University of Chicago Press, 2006)

Elaine Scarry, *The Body in Pain: The Making and Unmaking of the World* (New York: Oxford University Press, 1985)

Friedrich Schlegel, 'On Incomprehensibility', *Classic and Romantic German Aesthetics*, trans. P. Firchow, ed. J. M. Bernstein (Cambridge: Cambridge University Press, 2002)

Wallace Stevens, 'Adagia', *Opus Posthumous* (New York: Alfred A. Knopf, 1991)

Wallace Stevens, *Notes Toward a Supreme Fiction*, *The Collected Poems* (New York: Knopf, 1990)

D. W. Winnicott, 'The Aims of Psycho-Analytical Treatment', *The Maturational Process and the Facilitating Environment* (London: Karnac, 2005)

D. W. Winnicott, 'The Capacity to Be Alone', ibid.

D. W. Winnicott, 'Communicating and Not Communicating Leading to a Study of Certain Opposites', ibid.

D. W. Winnicott, 'Creativity and Its Origins', *Playing and Reality* (Hove: Brunner-Routledge, 1999)

D. W. Winnicott, 'Ego Integration in Child Development', *The Maturational Process and the Facilitating Environment*

D. W. Winnicott, 'Further Thoughts on Babies As Persons', *The Child, the Family and the Outside World* (London: Penguin, 1991)

D. W. Winnicott, 'Transitional Objects and Transitional Phenomena', *Playing and Reality*

Virginia Woolf, *A Room of One's Own* (London: Penguin, 1992)

Acknowledgements

This book wouldn't have been conceived without the encouragement and insight of my exceptional editor, Bella Lacey, and has benefited immeasurably through the course of its writing from her receptive ear for big ideas and her unerring eye for small details. I've also enjoyed the invaluable editorial input of Max Porter, and the patience of Ka Bradley in fielding my many anxious queries about permissions. The manuscript was copy-edited with great efficiency and thoughtfulness by Lesley Levene. My agent Sarah Ballard and her assistant Zoe Ross have been consistently enthusiastic and supportive.

Among the many teachers and colleagues who have consistently helped inspire and nurture my psychoanalytic thinking, I must name Gregorio Kohon, Rosine Perelberg, Rosemary Davies, Joan Schachter, Anne Patterson, Francois Louw, Megan Virtue and Steven Groarke – to whom I owe special thanks for his characteristically subtle and incisive comments on the first draft of the book. I can only hope Julian Levinson, Amy Gadney, Angie Simon, Devorah Baum, Beth Guilding and Natania Rosenfeld, who each took the time to read the work in progress and give me the benefit of their insight, curiosity and imagination, all know the depth of my gratitude. Over many years at Goldsmiths, I've had the good fortune of friends and colleagues as stimulating as Rick Crownshaw, Caroline Blinder and Lucia Boldrini with whom to discuss the writers and thinkers that figure in this book, as well as kind and unfussy help from Blake Morrison.

Abigail Cohen remains my best reader, textual and otherwise, and Ethan, Reuben and Ira Cohen my most careful non-readers. This book is dedicated to them.

Permissions

All possible care has been taken to trace the rights holders and secure permission for the texts quoted in this book. The author would like to thank the following for permission to reproduce copyright material:

Index

Keep in touch with
Granta Books:

Visit grantabooks.com to discover more.

GRANTA